How to Find Information

Second Edition

How to Find Information

A guide for researchers

Second Edition

Sally Rumsey

 Open University Press

Open University Press
McGraw-Hill Education
McGraw-Hill House
Shoppenhangers Road
Maidenhead
Berkshire
England
SL6 2QL

email: enquiries@openup.co.uk
world wide web: www.openup.co.uk

and Two Penn Plaza, New York, NY 10121-2289, USA

First published 2008

A catalogue record of this book is available from the British Library

ISBN-13: 978 0 335 226313
ISBN-10: 0 335 226310

Library of Congress Cataloguing-in-Publication Data
CIP data applied for

Typeset by RefineCatch Limited, Bungay, Suffolk
Printed in the UK by Bell and Bain Ltd, Glasgow

The McGraw·Hill Companies

Contents

Figures

Tables

Abbreviations

AHRC	Arts and Humanities Research Council
APA	American Psychological Association
BBSRC	Biotechnology and Biological Sciences Research Council
BLDSC	British Library Document Supply Centre
BNB	British National Bibliography
BOPCRIS	British Official Publications Collaborative Reader Information Service
CD	Compact Disc
CD-ROM	Compact Disc – Read Only Memory
CLA	Copyright Licensing Agency
COPAC	CURL OPAC
CORDIS	Community Research and Development Information Service
COS	Community of Science
CSA	Cambridge Scientific Abstracts
CURL	Consortium of University Research Libraries
DAI	Dissertation Abstracts International
DCC	Digital Curation Centre
DDC	Dewey Decimal Classification
DOAJ	Directory of Open Access Journals
DOI	Digital Object Identifiers
DPC	Digital Preservation Coalition
DVD	Digital Versatile Disc
ESRC	Economic and Social Research Council
ETD	Electronic Theses and Dissertations
EU	European Union
FE	Further Education
HE	Higher Education
HERO	Higher Education Research Opportunities
HEFE	Higher Education Funding Council of England
HMSO	Her Majesty's Stationery Office
ICT	Information and communication technology
IE	Information Environment (JISC)
IEEE	Institute of Electrical and Electronics Engineers
ILL	Interlibrary Loan
IP	Intellectual Property or Internet Protocol
ISBN	International Standard Book Number

ISO	International Organization for Standardization
ISSN	International Standard Serial Number
JISC	Joint Information Systems Committee
JISC PAS	JISC Plagiarism Advisory Service
LC	Library of Congress
LCSH	Library of Congress Subject Headings
MeSH	Medical Subject Headings
MRC	Medical Research Council
NDLTD	Networked Digital Library of Theses and Dissertations
NERC	Natural Environment Research Council
NHS	National Health Service
OAI	Open Archives Initiative
ONS	Office for National Statistics
OPAC	Online Public Access Catalogue
OpenDOAR	Directory of Open Access Repositories
OPSI	Office of Public Sector Information
PC	Personal Computer
PDF	Portable Document Format
PhD	Doctor of Philosophy
PLoS	Public Library of Science
PRO	Public Record Office
RAE	Research Assessment Exercise
RCUK	Research Councils UK
RDN	Resource Discovery Network
RePEc	Research Papers in Economics
RIN	Research Information Network
RLG	Research Libraries Group
ROAR	Registry of Open Access Repositories
RSLG	Research Support Libraries Group
RSLP	Research Support Libraries Programme
SPARC	The Scholarly Publishing and Academic Resources Coalition
SSO	Single Sign On
STFC	Science and Technology Facilities Council
TNA	The National Archives
UKDA	UK Data Archive
UK-IPO	UK Intellectual Property Office
UKOP	UK Official Publications
URL	Uniform Resource Locator
VRE	Virtual Research Environment
WoK	Web of Knowledge (ISI Thomson)
WWW	World Wide Web

Foreword to the first edition

At the heart of the research enterprise lies an absolute requirement to discover what other material has been published on the topic under study. Despite this fact few practical manuals exist to help the newcomer, or the more experienced researcher, find their way through all the complexities and hurdles which exist. That is what makes the present book so valuable and I predict it will become an important adjunct on every researcher's desk. Rather like learning statistics what a researcher needs is a volume with practical advice that can be turned to on a regular basis.

The book is also timely since the provision of 'research information resources' through local research libraries in individual universities or research institutes, is under going great change, largely as a result of the electronic revolution. Much material can now be accessed directly at the desk top and – for the researcher – is proving a considerable boon. But there are dangers that published material will be missed and so access to search engines and databases is vital. It is here in particular that difficulties exist since few seamless means of identifying all the various sources exist. If one is fortunate then a single website will suffice but that is rare in any branch of research.

As one reads this book it becomes ever more apparent that strenuous efforts are needed to stitch together the various strands and that lies behind the recommendations to create a UK Research Libraries Network (RLN) which arose from the report of the Research Support Libraries Group. The RLN starts work, based at the British Library, in April 2004.

The aims of this network, of all the librarians across the world, and most importantly of this manual is to make the ever growing complexity easier to understand and to navigate.

Brian K. Follett
Chair of the UK Research Libraries Support Group

Preface

This book is primarily aimed at those undertaking academic research at post-doctoral, doctoral, and masters level, but will also be useful to those working on undergraduate projects. Those in research institutions or public sector bodies, information seekers in commercial settings (for example, a law firm) and professionals wishing to keep up to date in their subjects will also find it helpful, as will anyone faced with writing a report, advising members of an organization or using a commercial information centre.

What is information? In the context of this book, it is any resource such as a document, book, or other format required by the researcher that informs, and contributes to extending their knowledge. It may be bibliographic information necessary for tracking down documents. It may be data, a historical book, or a paper not yet given at a conference written by a subject specialist. It could be a list of online subject gateways compiled by someone with knowledge of the subject area. It might be in electronic or a tangible format. It could be about a specialized subject area or a common, everyday topic.

And what about information overload? This term is of cold comfort to someone working in a subject where little has been written or who cannot find or access the information they need for their research. It is the *relevance* of information that is crucial – the right information available from the most appropriate source at the right time.

Finding information is one thing: working out what information is required in the first place, knowing where to look for it, how to recognize it when it is discovered, how to get hold of it, and then what to do with it are equally necessary. This book works through the skills and tools required by the researcher to achieve these ends. It deals mainly with electronic services and resources, although other formats are included.

The content is built on the following framework:

- deciding what information is required
- finding details of what is available
- obtaining the required information
- managing and using that information

The building blocks for information seeking are explained and a controlled, logical approach to information gathering is expounded. Serendipity plays an important role in the discovery of interesting and relevant sources which begs the question, is information retrieval an art or a science? One can be logical and methodical to a point, but, because every situation is different, one cannot be completely prescriptive about the methods. The researcher's experience built up over a period of time coupled with some lateral thinking (and a pinch of luck) all add to the process.

Some online resources offer two types of search facility: simple and advanced. Advanced searching implies the construction of long, complex search queries incorporating numerous devices such as truncation and proximity symbols. Perhaps so. Alternatively, advanced searching can be defined as knowing how to articulate a problem, then search for, locate, and access relevant information using a broad spectrum of appropriate resources.

Although designed to be reasonably comprehensive, some topics are inevitably dealt with in more detail than others. However, I have attempted to include enough detail to give readers a good start in that topic. With so much overlap in some areas it has been difficult at times to divide the content into discrete headings. In addition, the book is generic, that is, not focused on one particular discipline. It is the underlying techniques that are the mainstay of the text, and so examples are drawn from many subjects. It is not a guidebook to using the Internet neither is it about the technical details of electronic resources.

Inevitably a book concerned with electronic resources directs the reader to websites. The ephemeral nature of the web is well known, but I have chosen to include selected sites despite the danger that some may disappear or change within the lifetime of the book. Web addresses are listed separately and indicated within the main text using superscript numbering.

This book grew out of efforts to improve library provision for researchers at the University of Surrey and, its then federal partner, the University of Surrey Roehampton (now Roehampton University). It is also the result of experience of working with academic staff and students in attempting to ease the sometimes painful task of finding the information required for research in diverse and often highly specialized fields.

There are vast differences in the confidence and expertise of researchers in their ability to find what they need. Some are extremely competent with a well developed knowledge of use of connectors and creating search queries. Others have muddled along, never having been formally enlightened as to how or where to look. Christopher West in his response to a report by the Research Support Libraries Group (RSLG 2003) noted that,

> the implication is that all HE researchers arrive, like Botticelli's *Venus*, fully-formed with advanced information skills and that they are then completely purposive and efficient in the investigation of their information environments. Everyone who works in HE libraries knows that this isn't the case, even for academic staff.
>
> (West 2002: 146)

This book goes some way towards rectifying this situation.

Has the situation changed since the first edition of this book was published? In some ways the situation has become much more complex: resources available via the Internet are more numerous, the Web itself has expanded, particularly with the popularity of what have become known as Web 2.0 services, and other resources such as institutional repositories and **e-books** are proliferating. To counter the difficulties of resource discovery and finding appropriate copies, mechanisms such as open URL linking and federated search are more prevalent. Also users are increasingly 'net savvy'. However, information literacy training is as popular as ever in HE and information professionals are providing even better developed courses and training for users. The difficulties of finding information have not been resolved: they have evolved and the skills described within this book to deal with the complexity of the current situation are as relevant as they were in 2004.

Sally Rumsey
Guildford, Surrey

Acknowledgements

I am grateful to the following for granting permission to quote extracts from their publications:

- Cambridge Scientific Abstracts for use of the record from *Sociological Abstracts*, published by ProQuest CSA in Chapter 6
- The Higher Education Funding Council of England (HEFCE) for use of quotations from the RSLG (Research Support Libraries Group) final report
- The RED (Roehampton Educational Development) Centre for allowing me to use their advice on plagiarism
- Richard Waller (editor) and authors at *Ariadne* (UKOLN online journal) for permission to use extracts from articles published in *Ariadne*

The book grew out of work on the *Researcher's Gateway*, a dedicated website at the University of Surrey, and the *Researcher's Companion*, an online tutorial in information retrieval for researchers. Development of this tutorial would not have been possible without the expert input from Academic Liaison Librarians and Academic Liaison Officers at the University Library, University of Surrey, and the Information Resource Centre at Roehampton University. I should particularly like to thank Julie Mills at Roehampton and also Nadine Bannister for being such a model research assistant and making collaborative work so straightforward, even when separated by 25 miles of the A3.

Jennifer Nordon, then Academic Services Manager and Deputy Head of Library Services at the University of Surrey, was a constant support, especially during the writing of this text.

Tom Korolewicz gave his valuable time to read and comment on the original manuscript, for which I am extremely grateful.

None of this would have been possible without Robert Hall, Head of Library Services at the University of Surrey, who offered encouragement and advice from the start, as well as reading and commenting on the manuscript of the first edition.

I should also like to thank Liz Lyon, Director of UKOLN, who gave me my first opportunities to work on library research projects.

1

The information gathering process

The process • The skills required • Defining the subject • Defining the purpose and scope of the research • Setting up and getting started • Plan of campaign

The process

The most successful information gathering operations require a great deal of thought and the ability to work through each stage methodically.

The process of information gathering comprises a series of steps. However, this process is an art rather than a science: the researcher may not follow all the steps for every enquiry; guidelines can be given, but circumstances may dictate changes in direction; the researcher will return to previous steps during the course of their investigations; serendipity will play a part.

The process of finding, accessing, and handling information can be summarized as follows:

- Analyzing the question or problem
- Defining the scope of the research and what information is required
- Identifying sources of that information (resource discovery)
- Finding where that information is stored (resource location)
- Gaining access to that information
- Ensuring that the information retrieved is (a) what is required, (b) reliable (and possibly (c) current)

- Managing searches and results
- Keeping up to date and monitoring new developments

Which can be further broken down into:

- analyze
- define
- identify/discover
- locate
- access
- evaluate
- manage
- update

Although summarized numerically, the process is more circular than linear for large projects because of the heuristic nature of the work and the need to supplement what has been found with new discoveries. (See Figure 1.1.)

The skills required

The research process can be carried out efficiently and effectively providing the researcher has the necessary skills. The principal skills required by the researcher are:

- analytical
- planning
- searching (to know how and where to search)
- evaluation
- organizational

This book is designed to encourage the development of expert information researching skills.

Defining the subject

It may seem obvious, but before starting research, it is vital that the researcher is clear about what it is they are setting out to achieve. The original title (or problem) may have been decided by a third party, or the researcher may have set their own topic. Either way, the researcher should check that the title is meaningful and unambiguous: if not, clarification is required (for those

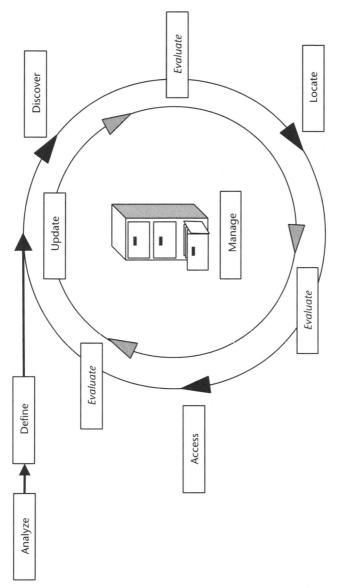

Figure 1.1 The information gathering process

undertaking doctoral research, a supervisor may offer guidance). It can be helpful to write down the title and work through the following, making changes as appropriate:

• Examine the words used: do they describe exactly what is being researched?
• Is there any ambiguity?
• Phrase the title/topic/main subject as a question (making sure the question retains relevance and covers all the areas intended); this can help the researcher define what it is they are actually doing.

Examples of titles and questions might be:

1 Title: Changes in the Russian manufacturing industry since the formation of the new Federation

  • What is the history and current state of the Russian manufacturing industry?
  • How has the Russian manufacturing industry changed since the formation of the new Federation?

2 Title: 'The evolution of hominid dietary adaptations linked with environmental changes: extending the record beyond 100,000 years' (Richards 2002).

  • Making reference to environmental changes, how has the hominid diet adapted and evolved beyond 100,000 years?
  • How have environmental changes affected the evolution of hominid dietary adaptations beyond 100,000 years?

3 Title: 'A pharmacy service for prisoners' (DoH and HMPS 2003).

  • What is the current situation regarding pharmacy services for prisoners and how might they be improved?

4 Title: 'Studies on the genomes of wild-type and vaccine strains of yellow fever virus' (Wang 1995).

  • What can we discover about the genomes of wild-type and vaccine strains of yellow fever virus?

The emphasis of the research will dictate the exact questions. The rewording of the original title into a question leads to further questions such as:

• What information will I need to be able to answer this question?
• Where will I find that information?
• How can I find out about other research in this subject area?

and so on. How to answers these and other questions will be dealt with in later chapters.

Defining the purpose and scope of the research

Answers to the following will have a bearing on how to handle the finding and accessing process. Spending some time considering these issues will help define the nature and extent of the research, which will then dictate how to plan and execute the information retrieval.

- What or who is the research for?
- What type of document will the finished product be (for example, doctoral **thesis**, company report)?
- What level of detail is necessary?
- Who will use or read the finished product?
- How much information is to be retrieved? Everything ever published on the topic? Key texts? A single **item**?
- How much time is available? Is this a large-scale, long-term project, a short essay, or something more immediate?
- How current does the information need to be? Legal information may need to be that which was made available this morning; an overview of a subject may consider historical changes over a period of time. Beware of outdated or discredited materials.
- How far would I be prepared to travel to access resources (specialist archives, records offices, museums, research libraries)?
- How much am I willing to spend (for example, the cost of document supply above any company or library allowance, travel, duplication and printing)?
- What am I entitled to use (for example, there may be access restrictions and other barriers such as those resulting from the Freedom of Information or Data Protection Acts)?
- Where do I start?

Setting up and getting started

The successful researcher will do their preparation before embarking on the main task. This will include investigations at the home library/ies:

- Finding out loan and other entitlements
- Obtaining a current library card or equivalent
- Obtaining any necessary usernames and passwords (see Chapter 2)
- Identifying an appropriate librarian or other individual who may be able to offer help

- Identifying available services (such as interlibrary loan or other document supply, or reciprocal borrowing arrangements at other libraries)
- Checking opening hours and other practicalities
- Finding out about the equipment (both hardware and software) needed to carry out the information seeking and management process:
  - checking Internet access
  - obtaining word processing and/or other software
  - accessing bibliographic software or other reference management system
  - printing facilities

The list of needs will depend on each individual case and should be compiled at the outset. Undoubtedly, needs will change during the course of the work, but having the basics available and functioning from the start can save problems later on.

Plan of campaign

The planning for information gathering can be likened to a military operation. A general might gather intelligence reports from informers, identify the strategic targets, plan the provision of food and transport and other facilities for the army, prepare a battle plan, review the situation hourly and act accordingly, and keep the commanders informed of the current and future situations. Similar tasks can be undertaken by a researcher for a successful and comprehensive outcome: meticulous planning, reviewing, and updating. This military style planning can be vital; stumbling across appropriate information is possible and can retrieve welcome sources, but not reliable. Figure 1.2 shows the information gathering process and how the different stages interrelate.

As stated above, the process will vary depending on the nature and extent of the research. For example, a person requiring a brief overview of a topic will probably want to identify and obtain a small number of key sources in a short time period. They may omit certain stages of the full process.

An important aspect of the information searching and retrieval process that needs stressing is its iterative (that is, repeating the process) and heuristic (that is, finding out as the process progresses and learning from what is discovered) nature. The more the researcher discovers, the more it leads to other sources. The key is not to become side-tracked into areas outside the remit, but remain on-task and follow up only relevant leads. As time progresses and the situation changes, so the researcher should be able to adapt to and monitor the changing landscape.

Having defined the subject and information needs and made the necessary preparations for information gathering, the researcher is ready to begin.

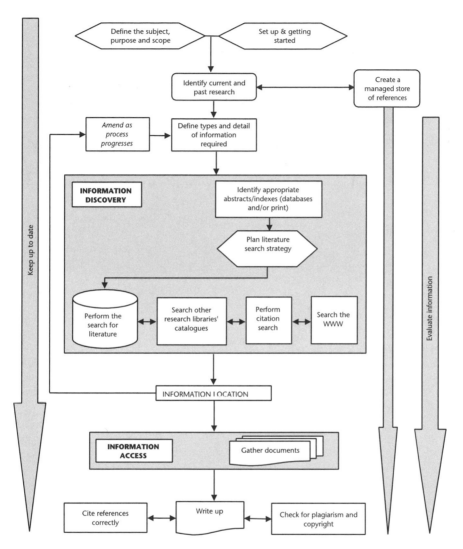

Figure 1.2 The researcher's information workflow

Key points

- Make sure the subject is clearly defined
- Be clear about both the purpose and the scope of the research
- Practicalities and other basic preparations should have been sorted out to ease the research process

> ### *Checklist*
>
> 1   Is the title/question clear and unambiguous? Are you clear what the research is about?
> 2   What is the purpose of the research? Who is the final product aimed at? Use the questions within the chapter to help define the purpose.
> 3   What is the scope and extent of the research? Use the questions within the chapter to help define the scope.
> 4   Have you dealt with all practicalities such as finding out usernames and passwords for electronic resources?

2

Making the most of a library

Getting to know your library and librarian

Getting to know your library and librarian

Introduction

Libraries range from those confined to an intimate room with a single member of staff to large, split-site collections being used by thousands of people. Whatever the type, the researcher needs to be able to find what is required efficiently. This demands an ability to use the facilities for scrutinizing the holdings and to locate the items required. It is necessary to know the services on offer and where to go or who to turn to for help.

A library by any other name

Since the mid-1980s there has been a move away from the traditional term 'library' in an attempt to reflect the other services and resources that these centres now offer. Some provide combined library and ICT (information and communication technology) services. Many libraries have abandoned the word and adopted terms such as:

- Learning resource centre
- Information service
- Learning centre

> In this book, the term 'library' is used to imply any department or centre that provides access to information for the purpose of research.

Orientation

Library staff may provide a personal tour of the building(s). An alternative may be a virtual tour, for example, using a video presentation. Whatever the method, it is advisable to become familiar with the building and collections of any library of which one is expecting to make repeated use.

Some libraries operate on multiple sites and users should find out about the method of movement of stock between the sites, the **collections** and the services offered by each site. There may be differences in opening times and in the specialisms of the staff as well as the collections.

Libraries vary in their provision of ICT resources and workstations. It may be necessary to log on using a network username and password: some may have computers with Internet access that are available to anyone. Some will provide laptop zones or wireless networking for use with personal portable computers. These are all issues that a visitor to a library may need to consider in order to make best use of the resources on offer.

Some university libraries provide a quiet section of the library with networked computers for the sole use of researchers. This has the advantage of being separated from the noise and bustle of the **open access** computers.

The emphasis of the collection

Although many libraries contain eclectic collections covering all or most subject areas in a variety of depths, many focus their collections on particular areas, defined by their users' interests. 'Libraries, we must never forget, are selections, defined by what they exclude' (MacColl 2006). There are those that build up archive collections and those that focus solely on current interests.

Specialist collections

There are a large number of specialist libraries comprising extensive collections in one or more subject areas. For example, the library of the London School of Economics is 'one of the largest libraries in the world devoted to the economic and social sciences' (LSE 2007) and the Wellcome Library for the History and Understanding of Medicine is 'one of the world's major resources for the study of medical history' (Wellcome Trust 2007a). Some retain small collections of rare materials which may not be available on open shelves, but researchers might be able to obtain access either via their own library or by making an appointment directly with the specialist library.

It is vital that researchers are aware of specialist collections in their subject field. A useful publication is the *Aslib Directory of Information Sources in the United Kingdom* (Reynard 2004) which gives details of information sources by subject area, has a comprehensive index, and includes contact details. Many large libraries stock this publication as well as others listing information sources in specific subject areas.

HERO (Higher Education & Research Opportunities)[1] provides links to libraries both in the UK and abroad (including many of those mentioned below) and the M25 Consortium[2] categorizes collections at participating libraries by subject. COPAC[3] academic and national library catalogue is a means of searching across the catalogues of multiple major research libraries in the UK using a single search page.

Legal deposit

There are six libraries that are entitled to a copy of every item published in the UK:

- The British Library[4]
- Bodleian Library,[5] Oxford
- National Library of Scotland,[6] Edinburgh
- National Library of Wales,[7] Aberystwyth
- Trinity College Library,[8] Dublin
- University Library,[9] Cambridge

Because of their extensive collections, these libraries can be of immense value to researchers, although there are restrictions on access (see also Chapter 11).

Unlike the other five who claim copies of items, publishers are obliged to send a copy of their publications to the British Library. Even though it is geographically in the Republic of Ireland, a historical agreement entitles Trinity College, Dublin, to the legal deposit of items published in the UK. There is no national library in Northern Ireland, a situation that is likely to continue for the foreseeable future, as the UK government dismissed the idea of creating a new legal deposit library in the province following a 1997 consultation paper.

The Legal Deposit Libraries Act 2003 (see: www.opsi.gov.uk/acts/acts2003/20030028.htm) updated previous legislation so that electronic publications will in future be included in the legal deposit process. This will add greatly to the scholarly literature and preserve a vast additional corpus of information.

The hybrid library

The library is predominantly a point of access to information, whether the information is in print, an audio recording, in digital format, or any other storage medium. Libraries' responsibilities extend to:

- Negotiating licensing agreements and subscriptions with database suppliers
- Arranging **document delivery** services with external bodies
- Managing and arranging collaborative access and borrowing schemes with other institutions
- Providing training (face to face and online) for users in using library resources
- Providing study space

and so on.

The library's presence on the Web

Most major libraries have large and comprehensive websites. These sites usually include details of resources and services and a link to the library's catalogue. However, not all smaller libraries have their own website. This means that the researcher who may be used to finding much of what they require on the WWW (World Wide Web), has to resort to use of the telephone, post, email, or a personal visit to find out more about the library and its collection(s).

A number of university libraries offer a section of their web pages dedicated to doctoral and post-doctoral researchers, for example, the Researcher's Gateway[10] at the University of Surrey.

Who to contact

For general enquiries there is usually some form of information desk or help-desk. Alternatively, many queries can be answered using the library's website or information leaflets.

Any researcher who uses one or more libraries frequently would be well advised to get to know an appropriate member of staff. This might be a librarian with knowledge of resources available in a particular subject area. Some libraries appoint a member of staff as research support librarian whose job it is to concentrate solely on library provision for researchers.

The researcher may be able to spend some time with the librarian, discussing their personal information requirements and obtaining advice regarding the availability and use of library resources. The librarian will be aware of other sources of information, outside the home library, in their subject area(s).

The titles of librarians vary between institutions. Researchers may come across the following: subject librarian, information professional, learning advisor, liaison librarian, information officer, resources officer, or other variation.

> In this book, the term 'librarian' is used for any information professional who advises researchers.

Helpdesk/information desk

All libraries have some form of help service for their users. This may take the form of a permanently staffed information desk, a Frequently Asked Questions kiosk, or library enquiry email service. If the library is run by a single person, it is unlikely that the librarian will be available to answer queries at all times. In a large library, an indepth reference query will often be referred to the appropriate specialist member of staff.

Training

Librarians are usually keen to help users find the information they require. Often this is by enabling them to find what they need for themselves. Being able to discover, access, and manage information efficiently and effectively is commonly called information literacy and the task of training users in these skills is usually the responsibility of librarians.

Because information is provided by an endless list of providers in a variety of formats via different interfaces, all researchers will benefit from advice from an information professional who specializes in information seeking and retrieval. It is recommended that researchers take advantage of any training available to them. Once learnt, these skills can be adapted to different settings and can save much time and frustration. Training in library and information skills may be included as part of a doctoral or other programme.

Free access versus authenticated access

The WWW enables convenient access to **electronic resources**. Libraries frequently have an impressive array of electronic resources to which they provide access. These may be databases, e-journals, e-books, datasets, or other materials. The benefits of electronic provision of these items include flexible and expert search options and access on and off site at any time. Access may be via **subscription**, be conditionally or **freely available**.

Just because a document is accessible via the Internet, does not imply that anyone is eligible to access it. Increasingly, reliable information is becoming freely available and there are many free information sources that are excellent in both content and organization (although there are others which are somewhat dubious). For example, the UK Government has made many of the publications and figures published by the UK National Statistics (ONS 2007) freely available on the WWW. However, for many commercial resources, the institution will pay a subscription on behalf of the user who has to prove their eligibility to access the information, usually by use of a username and password. **Licensing** terms are strict, and sanctions against institutions that contravene the agreement can be punitive, so libraries manage access arrangements carefully. These licensing agreements contain restrictions such as:

- The user may not be able to use the database for any commercial use if the agreement is for educational use only (this can include students who go on industrial placements and still have access to their university/college electronic resources).
- Publication of passwords to a third party is not allowed.
- The licence covers members of the named institution, so even if a researcher pays to join another library as an external member, they might not be able to access many electronic resources.
- Use is limited to a set number of **concurrent users**. When this limit is exceeded, other users cannot access the resource until someone logs off.
- Depending on the format and/or the licensing agreement, access may be limited to on site users.

Libraries and information centres select electronic resources which are relevant to their users and which they can afford.

A word about passwords

Passwords can be a source of frustration and confusion to users. Their use abounds, not only in the research seeking world, but life in general. One of the main problems is that of having to cope with many different passwords. The **Athens** system, which has been in use in UK higher and further education and other bodies, attempts to address this problem by providing a single username and password as a means of access to multiple compliant resources. A new system introduced into HE in 2006 and likely to be used for many online licenced resources means that users will be asked for their institutional logon details for many resources, which simplifies the situation further.

Logging on is becoming more streamlined as Single Sign On (SSO) gains popularity with information providers. This means that the user can sign on to a resource using their username and password, but does not have to repeat this process when transferring to another compliant resource in the same session.

Not all resources are authenticated by institutional login or Athens, so users often have to cope with other specially set passwords. These passwords can be difficult to manage as they have to be available for consultation by eligible users, but remain secret to everyone else. This can result in having to provide a password to find out what the correct password is for a resource! These passwords need changing regularly so that the resource remains accessible only to those who have the right of access.

Further help in using a library

For tips on how to search the library catalogue and other library hints see Appendix 1 which includes sections on:

- Library resources
- Library services
- The organization of information in a library
- Using a library catalogue

Key points

- Spend time becoming familiar with the library, its layout, resources, services, and the staff who are able to offer help
- Learn how to use the library catalogue effectively

Checklist

1   Do you know where in your library to find the printed resources for your research?
2   What relevant online resources are available to you at your home library?
3   Do you know how to access the online resources you need? Do you need a special password?
4   Are there specialist collections at other libraries that you should investigate?
5   Have you identified and met any library staff who will be able to help you with your research?
6   Is there any training in using library resources available?
7   Are you familiar with:

   - the classification system?
   - the catalogue and how to use it efficiently and effectively; are you aware of the limits of a library catalogue?
   - any specialist library services you may require?

If not see Appendix 1.

3

Finding information about existing research

The type of research referred to in this chapter • Access to information about research • Indexes and online databases of research activity • Research Councils UK and other funding bodies • Theses

The type of research referred to in this chapter

The research with which this chapter deals is that which is undertaken in academic institutions and/or funded by a major research funding body such as one of the UK Research Councils. Other research may be that which is ongoing in commercial companies or registered charities. One of the problems with much research activity is that the publications associated with it are not formally published and may not be available via commercial channels (grey literature: see Chapter 10 and Appendix 2).

This chapter is concerned with publications and sources that provide bibliographic details of research materials produced as a result of research. Another means of finding information about research is by citation searching (see Chapter 7).

Access to information about research

Details of research can be difficult to obtain and perhaps may not be in the public domain. The reasons for this may be:

- it is restricted company information (for example, information about new products)
- it contains sensitive information (for example, about an individual)
- it may be considered to have legal implications
- it may not have been published using the normal channels

Details can be found in scholarly publications such as published theses, journal articles, conference papers, pre-prints, or reports. There are indexes and directories available to aid the discovery of research activity. Some sources rely on the researchers themselves submitting details. This assumes that they are (a) aware of the index and (b) wish to have details made public. Others are maintained by institutions such as a research library and some obtain information directly from institutions.

Anyone undertaking doctoral or other high level research must first be sure that what they intend doing is original. They will wish to find out about other research activity in the subject area in order to inform their own work. There are initiatives around the world attempting to make research data and other materials more visible, accessible and re-useable. Some are national projects while others have been set up by individuals or commercial companies. The Web has enabled information about research to be potentially available to anyone with Internet access. However, there is neither a coordinated global index nor any national index that can be described as comprehensive.

Indexes and online databases of research activity

Commonwealth Universities Yearbook

This is an annual publication from the ACU (Association of Commonwealth Universities) and contains over 34,000 'departmental research entries' (Turner and Elmes 2006). It includes information about research centres, institutional data, and contact details and its coverage is around 500 universities in 36 countries throughout the Commonwealth. There are staff lists for each university including research staff and directors of research and summaries of main research areas for each department.

Community of Science (COS)

The COS[1] is a web network that offers services to researchers such as profiles of other researchers (those that have submitted their records) and research institutions, an up to date record of funding opportunities, and information about conferences. Institutions, corporations, and individuals can join the COS. Its success is dependent on the building of the community by the contributors. Subscribers can search for details of researchers (via the COS Expertise database) and research projects (via the COS Funded Research database). These databases can be searched by keyword, geography, and other options.

There are many hundreds of thousands of scientists and scholars who are members of the COS from over 1300 institutions across the world.

CORDIS (Community Research & Development Information Service)

CORDIS[2] is the research and development gateway of the European Union (EU) which provides information about EU funded research. It includes details of current and past projects, results, and publications in the Research and Technical Development (RTD) publications database, available via the online library. This database, accessible via the CORDIS website, holds records of publications from 1986. The research is undertaken by bodies such as commercial organizations, research institutes, or universities. The service offers advanced and professional search facilities for which the user may obtain free access, but must first register.

CORDIS offers opportunities to search for news about breakthroughs in EU research, the Technology Marketplace facilitates access to latest research results and the CORDIS library allows the downloading of research and development documents, conference papers, project reports, and other publications.

Examples of other databases of research activity

There are a number of online databases of research publications such as PhD-Data.[3] These are variable in their content and search facilities and some do not show their provenance or ownership. Although they can be a useful resource for finding out about research activity, users should be aware that (a) they may run on a commercial basis, (b) entries are submitted by the authors with no verification, and (c) they are not comprehensive.

NHS National Research Register[4]

This register of research projects is updated every three months and includes 'ongoing and recently completed research projects funded by, or of interest to, the United Kingdom's National Health Service (NHS)' (DoH 2007). Records dating from 2000 are included.

Current Legal Research Topics Database project

An interesting development is the provision of the Current Legal Research Topics Database at the IALS (Institute of Advance Legal Studies, University of London). The database is designed to provide a 'comprehensive listing of legal research currently undertaken in British law schools at MPhil (Master of Philosophy) or PhD (Doctor of Philosophy) level' (IALS 2002) and is aimed at postgraduate students and their research supervisors. It gives a brief record, with no contact details, but provides a useful service for those wishing to find titles of research which is underway, but not complete.

National Research Register for Social Care

This recently initiated register 'will capture all research carried out within, or commissioned by, local Councils with Social Services Responsibilities (CSSRs)' (SCIE 2007). The register is under development.

Research Councils UK and other funding bodies

The UK research councils

Research Councils UK (RCUK) is a 'strategic partnership of the UK's seven research councils' (RCUK 2007). The councils fund research projects whose details are available via the RCUK. Users may search the research councils' databases which provide brief details of current or recently funded research.

The seven research councils are listed below and each publishes information about the research it has funded. Some maintain databases of research activities.

- AHRC: Arts and Humanities Research Council. Details of awards made are under *Award listings*.
- BBSRC: the Biotechnology and Biological Sciences Research Council. The BBSRC online database of research is named Oasis[5].
- EPSRC: The Engineering and Physical Sciences Research Council. Details are maintained on the *Funded Grants on the Web* pages.
- ESRC: Economic and Social Research Council. The council website, *ESRC Society Today*, 'will offer a broad picture of the research available, both planned and in progress around particular social science subjects. As well as bringing together all ESRC-funded research, it is strongly hoped that ESRC Society Today will act as a gateway to other key online resources' (ESRC 2007).
- MRC: Medical Research Council. A database of research activity should be available from summer 2007.
- NERC: Natural Environment Research Council. A database of funded research, with links to many of the projects, is available on the *Grants on the Web* (GOTW) pages.
- STFC: Science and Technology Facilities Council (formed in April 2007 by a merger of the PPARC (Particle Physics and Astronomy Research

Council) and CCLRC (Council for the Central Laboratory of the Research Councils)).

The HERO[6] website provides links to the research councils and information about research activity in the UK.

Other bodies and funding institutions

There are many other bodies undertaking and funding research. They include charitable and other foundations, national and internationally funded bodies and learned societies. Details of such bodies might be found in a publication such as *The Grants Register* (Palgrave Macmillan 2007).

University departments

Most universities provide limited information regarding the research currently taking place in their departments. Finding out what is current at each university is difficult without knowing likely sites where research into a specific subject area may be taking place.

Charitable organizations

Charitable organizations often work in tandem with or directly fund research that takes place in HE. Medical charities may work with scientists in research hospitals; other charities run research projects themselves. Larger charities, such as the Wellcome Trust, the Institute of Cancer Research, the Joseph Rowntree Foundation, and Action Research, often provide details of research projects and resulting publications on their websites.

Theses

Doctoral theses and dissertations

A doctoral thesis is a published work resulting from research that makes a significant and original contribution to the advancement of knowledge. It is awarded by an HE establishment and the successful candidate is entitled to append the letters PhD, or similar, to their name. In the UK these publications are generally called theses, but in the US, dissertations, a word generally reserved for taught postgraduate and undergraduate projects in the UK.

There are a number of routes for obtaining details of theses. In the UK, *Index to Theses* (Expert Information 2007) and the British Library are the major sources of information (see below). Theses from other nations may be more problematic. *Dissertations Abstracts International* is a publication that lists details and abstracts of theses from the US and other countries (see below). Occasionally, doctoral theses are published commercially and in these cases, there should be a bibliographic record.

Increasingly the full text of theses is being made available online. In the UK a new model, EThOS, for online thesis provision is in preparation at the time of writing and is set to provide a central hub which provides not only a bibliographic record of completed theses, but also the means of delivering the full text.

Masters dissertations are not indexed in the same way as doctoral theses. This makes identification more difficult. It should be noted that information contained in these publications is not necessarily original research and institutions may retain copies for a limited period.

British Library and EThOS

Records of British theses held in the BL's collection and available via the British Thesis Service[7] can be searched using the *Document Supply Material* section of the *Integrated Catalogue*. This service is due to be replaced by the new online service, EThOS: at the time of writing (June 2007) exact details are yet to be released.

Index to theses

This index allows the user to search for higher degrees accepted by the universities of Great Britain and Ireland (Expert Information 2007). It relies on the submission of details of works by the universities. It is available both in print and online (by subscription) and can be searched by author, keyword, title, or subject. The 1716–1950: The Retrospective Index to Theses comprises bibliographic listings only and *Index to theses* (from 1950) includes many abstracts from 1970 onwards. The time from submission until publication takes around three months.

ProQuest Dissertations and Theses Database

This subscription database, published by the US publisher UMI,[8] holds the details of over 2.3 million doctoral and masters theses and dissertations. Coverage begins in 1861 and entries from 1980 include an abstract. The emphasis is on US publications. Over 750,000 titles are available full text electronically.

Individual academic institutions

University libraries catalogue the theses that they hold in stock. A search to find publications in this way can be laborious if the researcher has no knowledge of likely sites in a given subject area.

Increasingly, academic institutions are providing free online access to many of their theses. Sometimes they can be found on the relevant departmental website, but as institutional repositories are growing, more of them are being stored and delivered in this way.

Key points

- Researchers need to find details of current and past research to inform their own work
- Obtaining details may be difficult as much of the corpus is grey literature

---

Checklist

1   Have you checked indexes and databases of current research?
2   Have you found out about current research funded by funding agencies and other bodies?
3   Have you identified relevant theses?

4

The type and detail of information required

Introduction • Types of information • Primary and secondary sources
• Multidisciplinarity and subject overlap • Defining the area and limits of
the research • How much information is appropriate? • What is already
known? • Planning an information finding strategy

Introduction

Before setting out to find information, it is important to have a plan of what is
(and is not) needed. Obviously, the researcher cannot include things of which
they are not aware, but an initial outline of the requirements can be created
using the most basic knowledge. Reading around and talking to others who
have some knowledge of the topic are good starting points for getting a feel for
the subject. It is helpful to join appropriate mailing lists and alerting services
(see Chapter 15) in order to gather relevant information and monitor current
activity. As the project continues, the researcher's journey will enable them to
add to their knowledge of sources of information. They will also reject sources
and items which may at first have seemed vital.

Having set up the mechanisms for obtaining information as given in
Chapter 1 and carefully defined the question or problem, the researcher is
ready to move on to the next stage of information gathering process: defining
what information is required.

Types of information

If the researcher is writing a short essay or report, it may be sufficient to access some key books and journal articles and no other documents. It can, however, become rapidly apparent that more might be necessary. A researcher investigating, for example, the status of women in the workplace may want to quote sections from documents that add weight to the discussion such as the Equal Pay Act 1970 or government statistics of women's earnings during a particular period. Such information can then be used to support an argument or prove the historical context.

Researchers should consider carefully all the information sources relevant to their work (of which they are aware) before embarking on the search. Needs may change as the research progresses: for example, encyclopaedias are useful for an overview at the outset, but later on, more specialist and detailed information will be needed. Or the researcher may read conflicting reports of a situation and decide to access the primary information to ascertain which is the more accurate.

The researcher should therefore decide:

1 What formats of information are likely to be required (see Appendix 2)
2 What types of documents within those formats will be needed (for example, the minutes of meetings, dictionaries, parish records, journal articles, videos of a performance, original dataset)
3 Whether primary and/or secondary sources will be necessary (see below)

Numbers 2 and 3 should be considered together.

Some examples of types of documents or information might be:

- chapters of books
- journal articles
- newspaper articles
- websites
- statistics publications
- official government publications
- datasets (raw data and processed data)
- leaflets
- theses
- conference proceedings
- the general public
- specialists in the subject area
- audio visual materials
- company reports
- standards

- local or national records (for example, council, genealogical or planning records)

There may be issues with some of these publications such as the length of time between data gathering and publication (see Appendix 2).

Primary and secondary sources

Much research demands that the researcher access both primary and secondary sources of information. To define the two types of sources:

1 A primary source is one that is a record of events as they are first recorded without analysis or commentary. It may be a set of data, such as census statistics, that has been set out in an orderly fashion, but not interpreted. It may be first hand accounts or direct evidence of an event or item. Original research often requires primary sources. For example:

   - A music scholar may return to original manuscripts to clarify exactly what the composer wrote
   - A medical researcher may wish to access data about a drugs trial to ascertain the effects of that drug
   - A researcher investigating an event may wish to read diaries and letters of those involved

2 A secondary source is one that interprets or analyses an event or phenomenon. It often attempts to describe or explain primary sources. A secondary source such as a textbook may include some primary sources as examples. Examples of the uses of secondary sources might be:

   - The music scholar will obtain articles and commentaries on the work in question to gauge the opinions of other scholars
   - The medical researcher reads journal articles on the disease in question to find the experiences of others working in the field
   - The historical researcher will access texts of other scholars' interpretations of the event

For some types of research it is imperative to access the primary data. These data provide the building blocks upon which all analysis and interpretation is created. The researcher may know that they need to access primary sources before they set out looking for information, even if they are not sure exactly what the item is that they require. If secondary sources are required, they will need to consider the types of resources appropriate for the project.

Multidisciplinarity and subject overlap

Although much work takes place in a single broad subject area other research involves two or more disciplines. In fact, 'research is becoming increasingly multi-disciplinary and inter-disciplinary' (BBSRC 2007). This is often as a result of collaboration or a new perspective on a problem. For example, there are researchers working in areas such as psychoacoustics (the partnership of the perception and science of sound), gender issues in the French media (a mixture of sociology and language), or crop science (including the topics of plant science, pests and disease-causing organisms, bio-fuels, pesticides, and drought). There is an increasing emphasis on research at the border between disciplines, especially with developments in new technologies.

On a narrower level, work may overlap between two or more areas in the same basic discipline, for example, machine translation and linguistics.

The individual seeking information for research will therefore have to clarify from which angle(s) they are approaching the topic and identify areas where there is any subject overlap. If this is the case, a researcher familiar with information sources in one subject area, may need to use those of another.

Defining the area and limits of the research

Setting boundaries in both breadth and depth of the chosen topic will maintain the research within the defined topic. The researcher should be clear about the area(s) that is/are included, and equally about what will not be included. This can be achieved by setting limits. Doing this will:

- Enable decisions on where to stop gathering information
- Help to ascertain whether or not information is pertinent
- Keep the research focused therefore avoiding creeping growth resulting in an unmanageably large project

For example, a researcher concerned with voter apathy in elections may wish to decide:

- Which country/ies to investigate (and therefore which to exclude)
- The types of election (political – general, local; other types of election such as trades union)
- Whether the research concerns certain age groups or other category of voter (and therefore which will be ignored)
- Whether attitudes towards political parties will include all parties, a selected number, or be treated as a more general issue

- What to include regarding related factors such as trades unions, career politicians, and the influence of the media. Decisions should be made about which factors will be investigated and which not
- The time factor, that is, setting a range of dates which the research will cover. For example, any elections regardless of date; all elections held during the twentieth century; the 1997 UK General Election

This is a general example, but illustrates the point that if limits are not set, the research can quickly expand into additional vast areas, resulting in loss of focus and a badly defined research topic. In essence, the researcher is defining what can be considered relevant material.

How much information is appropriate?

Deciding the amount of information to gather is a difficult question to answer but one which the researcher should consider. The quantity required will be dictated largely by the nature of the research being undertaken, for example a short report, a doctoral thesis, a journal article, and the time available. See the section in Chapter 1, defining the purpose and scope of the research.

What is already known?

While deciding what information is needed for the project, the researcher should document relevant sources of which they are already aware. Under the main subject areas or headings, list the sources already known where information may be found. This should include all sources: people (specialists in the field and personal contacts); publications; other sources such as records, audio visual materials and artefacts; organizations and other bodies; relevant sources of information such as indexes, websites, bibliographies, or online databases. Where appropriate, they may be checked for additional sources, for example, a book chapter may contain a list of references for other linked or related works.

Planning an information finding strategy

It might be worth spending a few minutes thinking about a general strategy for finding information for the project:

1 Background information: sources can include general, broad introductions or publications such as subject encyclopedias. How much background information do you need or do you have time to find and use?
2 What are the key sources in the subject? How are you going to identify them?
3 Is there anyone who can help you decide where to start?
4 Peripheral information. Do you have the time and does the project warrant large amounts of reading around the subject?
5 Do you need to find everything written on the topic or only major seminal works or something in between? You will need to be able to judge the importance of materials. Omitting to mention a key work on a topic could be disastrous.

Key points

- Decide whether or not it is likely that the research requires access to primary sources
- Have a clear idea of the types of resources that will be needed
- Think carefully about the quantity of information that is required for the project in hand.
- Find out about the main resources in other disciplines which are relevant for multidisciplinary work
- Define the scope of the research in detail to prevent 'research creep'
- Document what is already known

Checklist

1 What will the end product be: a brief resumé, a document of a few thousand words, or a large scale work such as a thesis, an in depth report, or a book?
2 How much research/time/information is appropriate for this type of work?
3 How much time is available for the project?
4 What types of materials will be required?
5 Will you need access to any difficult to obtain primary sources?
6 Are there sources of information in other disciplines which are relevant?
7 Have you set clear limits for the research? What are you *not* going to include? Where are the boundaries of the research?
8 Have you made a record of what is already known and relevant to this project?
9 Do you have a general idea of your information finding strategy?

5

Discovering relevant materials

Resource discovery: where details of relevant materials can be found
• What are abstracts and indexes? • Online bibliographic databases
• Issues relating to online databases • e-Books • Catalogues and
bibliographies • Open access materials • Other sources and types of
information • Selecting sources relevant to the subject

Resource discovery: where details of relevant materials can be found

Having identified what information is required, obtaining resources for research is a three-stage process:

- Resource discovery – that is, finding out what resources exist in the chosen topic area
- Resource location – finding out where those resources are stored
- Resource access – actually obtaining the item(s) in full text (or equivalent)

Information providers, bodies such as the JISC and librarians are working towards seamless online provision where the user discovers a resource and obtains immediate access to the most **appropriate copy** (i.e., the copy to which the researcher has the best access for the circumstances, e.g., fastest, nearest, and so on). Although this situation exists in some areas, (depending on subscriptions and service providers) it is not universal and it is probably necessary to work through the three steps of the process.

Resource discovery is the process of finding the details (bibliographic or otherwise) of existing resources that are relevant to the chosen topic. There are a number of sources available that enable the researcher to perform this task. In general they comprise abstracts and indexes, catalogues, and bibliographies, although there are other sources that can be tapped.

This chapter is concerned with *where* to look to discover resources and discusses the features of online databases. Chapter 6 gives details of *how* to search for resources.

What are abstracts and indexes?

Many journals provide an index to their contents, often published at the end of each year. Cumulative indexes are less common so, although useful, these annual indexes only include a single year's listings of the contents from one title. If no other source were available, the researcher intending to search more widely would be forced to peruse the indexes of all the titles of interest, a highly unsatisfactory method of working. To resolve this situation, there are indexing services which compile indexes covering large numbers of titles. For example, the *Biography Index* contains bibliographical information from over 3000 journals and 2000 books for individuals and groups in all subjects. *Historical Abstracts* performs a similar function for articles in the subject area of history and includes references from over 2000 journals. There are broad publications that cover interdisciplinary subjects, such as *Scopus* which includes life, health, physical, and social sciences and *IBSS (International Bibliography of the Social Sciences)*.

Indexes may provide only the bibliographic details of the articles, while abstracting services also include a summary of the article. Confusingly, indexes also sometimes contain abstracts (see, for example, *Index to Theses*). The presence of an abstract enables the researcher to be more discerning in their selection of articles, as they have a better concept of the content.

Some collections have been in publication for many years, for example the *Chemical Abstracts Service* (CAS) has indexed and summarized chemistry related articles from many tens of thousands of scientific journals since 1907. in addition it provides details of patents, conference proceedings, and other documents pertinent to chemistry, life sciences, and other scientific fields. This service, which provides abstracts for more than 27 million documents, is available to subscribers online.

Like *Chemical Abstracts*, many publishers provide an online service with well designed access and search options. Performing a search using a printed version is time consuming and can create a complex search trail that the researcher must be diligent in managing. An online service allows the researcher to perform keyword searches within the text of the abstract and to search other fields such as indexing terms (or descriptors) and author affiliation (although this can have its difficulties). Coupled with this, users can manage their searches and results efficiently and are often able to set up search alerts (see Chapter 15).

Online bibliographic databases

An online bibliographic database is an electronic store of bibliographic information about journal articles and sometimes other resources such as book reviews, reports, and conference proceedings. They are most frequently accessed via the WWW although some are available on CD-ROM (and networked in some institutions), A web-based database can be updated easily and access via the Internet is preferable for users.

It is true that good quality information on the WWW can be found using a search engine, however most of the valuable information contained in these databases will not be discovered by that method. Subscribers to online databases pay for:

- The well ordered structure of the database
- The ability to search in a structured fashion
- The specialist content of the database
- The indexing and thesaurus construction

Most of the large printed indexes and abstracting services have an online version either running in tandem with the printed publication, or replacing it completely. Another benefit of the Internet database is that, in many cases, there are additional live links and facilities on the database not possible in a print version of the same publication such as linking seamlessly from references to full text and download selected records or bibliographic details.

Databases are often supplied through a commercial agent such as Ovid or ProQuest CSA. It is usually possible to search across all or some of the databases on offer at one time. Users pay a subscription and are required to sign a licence (usually paid for and signed by their institution; see Chapter 2).

The records held on bibliographic databases

The records held on bibliographic databases contain information similar to that included in printed abstracts and indexes. However, the distinction between those that supply only bibliographic information and abstracts, and those that supply full text is becoming blurred. As agreements and deals are made between publishers, particularly with initiatives such as CrossRef,[1] together with work on the Information Environment and open URLS (see Chapter 16), many are providing seamless links to full text at a separate site.

A database such as IngentaConnect[2] is one where the user can access the full text of the journals to which their institution has subscribed, but is able to search the database for records, including abstracts, of other works (and can then find the full text via another source). This chapter is concerned with finding bibliographic details and abstracts; full text access is dealt with in Chapter 10.

The entry for each item on the database is called a record and each record contains bibliographic information stored in named fields. The fields may include:

- author(s)
- title (of article)
- source (publication where the article was published)
- volume
- issue/part number
- date of publication
- date of addition to database
- abstract
- major descriptors/subject headings
- minor descriptors/subject headings

For example, the record in Figure 5.1 was retrieved using *Sociological Abstracts* via ProQuest CSA (Cambridge Scientific Abstracts).

Each of the fields may be searched and the authors' names are linked to other records by the same authors on the database. Bold text indicates the search terms used to retrieve the record. The descriptors can be used to search again, either broadening or narrowing the search.

Issues relating to online databases

Although the principles of searching structured databases are the same, each has its individual features. Some are simple in that the options for searching are few, but easy to use. Others are more complex but permit targeted search strategies. Even basic features differ and it is advisable to check the features using the 'Help' function. The database is only as good as the information it is given. If the search query is not acceptable to the database, it will produce unsatisfactory or even no results.

Content and coverage

A database will often include a list of:

- The subject matter covered by the database
- The serials indexed by the database

Database	ProQuest CSA Sociological Abstracts
Title	Class Matters: The Persisting Effects of Contextual Social Class on Individual Voting in Britain, 1964-97
Author	Andersen, Robert; Heath, Anthony
Affiliation	Dept Sociology, U Oxford, UK
Source	European Sociological Review, vol. 18, no. 2, pp. 125-138, June 2002
ISSN	0266-7215
Descriptors	*Social Class *Voting Behavior *United Kingdom *Class Differences

New Search Using Marked Terms: Use AND to narrow   Use OR to broaden

Abstract   This paper extends previous work on the changing importance of individual & contextual social class in GB. We adopt a multilevel framework for analysis, linking surveys from the 1964-1997 British Election Studies with Census data on the social-class composition of constituencies. The goal of the paper is to test whether, net of individual social-class effects, the social-class composition of the constituency in which the voter lives has declined in importance over time. We found that contextual class effects were consistently significant & fairly constant throughout the period under study. We also find a gradual increase in the amount of constituency variation in vote. Although the proportion of this variation explained by contextual & individual social class has remained fairly constant for Conservative vote, it has decreased for Labour vote. Ultimately, we find evidence of a decline in class voting, but no evidence of a growth in the individualism of voters. 3 Tables, 5 Figures, 1 Appendix, 50 References. Adapted from the source document.

CODEN	ESOREP
Language	English
Publication Year	2002
Publication Type	Journal Article
Classification	0925 political sociology/interactions; sociology of political systems, politics, & power
Update	20070401
Accession Number	200216413
Journal Volume	18
Journal Issue	2
Journal Pages	125-138
Country of Publication	United Kingdom

Reproduced with permission from ProQuest CSA

Figure 5.1 Example of a bibliographic record

This information can be of great value for ascertaining whether or not it is worthwhile using the database in question. If it is not available, it may be obtainable from the database provider. For example, the APA (American Psychological Association)[3] that produces the PsychINFO database provides a list of the journals indexed, plus other relevant information about the content.

Another aspect of database content that is of interest is the date of coverage. This could have a bearing on other sources the searcher wishes to access if, for example, the coverage timescale does not include all that is required. Some databases do not index articles as far back as others. Some include historical information, but the older the information, the more incomplete it may be. The researcher may find that the database extends further back in time for records with citation details than it does for those with abstracts.

Compare the date ranges of the following databases:

- Bioengineering Abstracts from 1993
- Legal Journals Index (via Westlaw) from 1986
- Art Abstracts from 1984
- Conference Papers Index from 1982
- Linguistics & Language Behavior Abstracts from 1973
- Econlit from 1969
- Inspec from 1969 and Inspec Archive 1898–1968
- IBSS – *International Bibliography of Social Sciences* from 1951
- PsychINFO from 1887

Many database providers are now creating additional databases of archive materials (see for example, Inspec above) which cover a specified static period.

The researcher may wish to check frequency of updating, particularly if they are concerned that they are accessing the most up to date information.

Searching options of an online database

Not all databases include all of the following options. Being aware of such issues and features means that the database can be used to its fullest capacity.

Case sensitivity

Most databases are not case sensitive. The legal databases tend not to require standard punctuation when searching using a legal citation.

Structured search queries

Most databases require the use of structured searching: it is beneficial to learn searching skills (see Chapter 6). A structured search may be aided by the provision of search boxes. A properly constructed query enables the searcher to be specific about the information they retrieve.

Quick search versus advanced search

Most databases offer a choice between quick and advanced search. Quick search is useful when an overview is required and the searcher is unconcerned about the numbers of records retrieved. It can also be useful when searching using a narrow term or unusual name (both unlikely to retrieve large numbers of records). The advanced option allows a more precise search, often with comprehensive limiting options.

The search interface

The search interface of a database may offer one or more of the following options:

- A free text box allowing the searcher to type in exactly the search query they require (in a box labelled 'Command-line search', 'terms and connectors' or similar)
- Boxes for the searcher to type in their terms, linked by **Boolean operators**, often in drop down menus
- Boxes for terms preceded by instructions such as 'including all the terms', 'including some of the terms', or 'including the exact phrase'

See Chapter 6 for details of searching using Boolean logic and other operators.

Searching in specific fields

Databases are constructed with relevant information assigned to set fields (see Table 5.1). Searching using specified fields gives a great degree of flexibility and accuracy. This can be achieved by either selecting the field required from a drop down menu or by including the field abbreviation in the search query. For example,

---

Typing the query:

- Greenfield in AU

or

- 'business accounting' in SO

when searching for a particular author or source.

A search within the title field can produce results that are more relevant than searching the entire record or abstract. This is because the item is likely to be about that subject rather than mention it as part of a broader topic and is a good means of narrowing down a search. For example, compare the numbers of results shown in Table 5.1.

Table 5.1 Comparison of searches in different fields

Field	Numbers of records retrieved
Keyword	14,455
Descriptors	13,342
Abstract	2,324
Title	874

Note: Search query, 'discourse analysis'

Source: Search run on *Linguistics and Language Behavior Abstracts*, 4.11.07

It is often possible to select the type of publication in which to run the search (for example, journal articles, conference proceedings, or reports). Narrowing down the search in this way helps focus the results.

Searching using the title of a known journal can be useful for:

- Finding records of articles to which the searcher knows they have access; the name of the journal can be combined with additional terms to retrieve articles on a chosen topic
- Keeping up to date with the contents of a preferred journal

The user may be able to select the journal from a given list or type in the title and search the source field.

Thesaurus search

If a database includes a thesaurus, the searcher is well advised to make use of it. Running a search on a database's own thesaurus can help selection of terms that have been indexed in that database. It also serves to suggest related, broader, and narrower terms as well as indicating preferred terms. Terms may have a scope (or explanatory) note giving details of their meaning in the context of the database. The terms in the thesaurus may have live links for easy searching.

Some databases include recognized subject headings as search options. For example, Medline includes MeSH subject headings in its controlled vocabulary.

Index search

The index lists the indexed terms in alphabetical order. This can be useful when checking different forms of a word and for browsing. As with thesaurus terms, it may be possible to run a search using a particular term by clicking on a live link.

Related reference search

Some databases (and OPACs) offer an option to retrieve related references, that is, records on the same topic as that which has been retrieved. This is a useful facility, as relevant records can be obtained that may not have been picked up by the search query and might otherwise have been missed.

The Web of Science database offers this function. For example, the records retrieved from a search using the query:

multiple sclerosis AND cannabis

includes a reference to:

Killestein J., Uitdehaag, B.M.J., and Polman, C.H. (2004) Cannabinoids in multiple sclerosis – Do they have a therapeutic role? *Drugs*, 64(1): 1–11.

Running a search using the 'Find related records' option results in a number of hits including:

Pacher, P., Batkai, S., and Kunos, G. (2006) The endocannabinoid system as an emerging target of pharmacotherapy, *Pharmacological Reviews*, September, 58(3): 389–462.

which was not retrieved in the first search.

Searching across multiple databases

Databases provided by a large supplier, such as CSA or Ovid, offer a selection of titles and may allow searches of more than one at a time. This option will produce more results, but will save time. A database such as Medline or PsycINFO comprises a number of smaller databases, divided by date range. In this case the user may select the date ranges most relevant to their search. When dealing with dates, users should be aware of whether the dates are those of the publication of the article, or the date the record was added to the database.

Searching across databases from different providers is becoming more common as the technology and standards are developed to enable this. Libraries may have a system known as a federated or cross-search system which allows the searcher to search across all or some of the databases to which that institutions has access. Although useful, including searching databases which may not have been considered, and time saving, there is a main pitfall: because all databases are slightly differently constructed, the search may not be as successful as searching within the native interface of each database. This conundrum is one which is exercising the information community. (See Chapter 16.)

Understanding records

Numbers of records retrieved

Monitoring the number of records retrieved is key to narrowing down a search to a manageable number of relevant results as the search is honed and relevance is increased. Or conversely, more records are retrieved in a narrow subject area. It can also alert the user to errors in their searching.

Sets

The word 'set' (or 'search number') is used to describe the results of one search query. The database may give the option to combine sets using Boolean operators, or a set may be selected for the query to be edited or added to in some way. The sets may be numbered using the hash symbol. In this case, the user may be able to type a search query using the set number. For example:

#3 AND (monsoon OR rains)

where set 3 was a previous query (such as Bangladesh OR India).

Changing the view

There may be options regarding the detail displayed in a list of results. A list of brief citations is useful when scanning results for relevance or quickly identifying records of possible interest. In order to evaluate the content of an article more accurately for relevance, the searcher will wish to access other fields such as the abstract and descriptors if they are available. They may be able to select the fields they wish to see displayed. Options that might be available are:

- Citation: brief details of author, title, publication, volume, issue, and date
- Citation and abstract: the above plus the abstract
- Full record: all the information included in the record
- Full record omit references: if a database includes references in the record, they can make the record lengthy

- KWIC (Key Word In Context): Short extracts from the record that include the keyword; useful when evaluating the relevance of a record. If a device such as truncation has been used, the searcher can easily identify any unexpected rogue words, or homographs, only one of which is relevant. The searcher can than edit the search to make the results more relevant.

Whatever the display selected, it is common to find the search terms displayed in bold or coloured type.

Records are usually displayed in reverse chronological order of date of publication (most recent first), but the user can often choose the way in which results are presented.

Navigating around the results

The searcher is usually able to navigate around the results by either scrolling using an arrow symbol (◄ ►), by specifying the number of the result they wish to display or by clicking on a 'next record' or 'previous record' button. Having displayed an individual record, there will be a button or link to return to the list of results.

There may be an option to search within the results, enabling the search to be narrowed down.

Links within the record

Terms within a record might be hyperlinked: clicking on them enables discovery of other records that include those terms. It is common to find these links for the

- author's name
- title of journal
- descriptors

Some of these options will result in large numbers of results, but it is a useful means of finding other records with similar characteristics, or articles by the same author.

Managing results

Marking records

Most databases allow users to mark (or tag) records using a check box or 'mark records' button. This means that the researcher can mark those records they have identified as being of most relevance, then click on the 'show marked records' button to strip out those not selected, leaving a shorter, apposite list.

Printing, saving, or emailing records

In order to manage research well, searchers should be diligent in keeping records of relevant references by saving them in some way. A printed or saved list is useful when visiting a library to track down sources. It is advisable to retain an electronic copy of references so that the text can be easily edited when creating a list of references or bibliography, saving time retyping the details. The electronic copy can be made either by downloading or by sending an email to oneself.

If using bibliographic software (see Chapter 13), results can sometimes be downloaded directly to the chosen package. If available, each database should be checked for the means of doing this.

There may be the option to select the sections of the record(s) for printing, saving or emailing, for example, saving entire records, or just citations and abstracts. It is often possible to select exactly which record(s) should be saved, for example, current record displayed, marked records, all records, or specific selected records.

Search history

Searches run in one session form a search history. This will be shown either on the search page where the search history can be seen building up with each subsequent search, or on a separate page. Using this facility, searches already performed in a session can be combined, edited or re-run.

The search history can be saved or printed which is valuable for record keeping purposes.

Saving searches

If searches in a session are saved, they can be revisited during a later session on that database. The results can be accessed or the search re-run to update it.

Alerts

Alerts are a means of keeping up to date (see Chapter 15).

Quirks

Because databases vary, the user should take care to notice any quirks associated with the one they are using. Their librarian will be able to help in this respect and will alert users to possible anomalies. For example, Science Direct requires that the search history facility is turned on *before* embarking on a search.

Logging off from a database using its own logging off button (when available) can be important, particularly if the licensing agreement is for a limited number of concurrent users. In such a case, not logging off can result in another user being unable to access the database for some time.

Help function

The 'Help' functions of databases vary from those which are comprehensive with an inbuilt search facility or index, to those which are of little use. However, the researcher should check the help available as it will engender more efficient use of the database and its functions.

e-Books

It is difficult to define exactly what is meant by the term 'e-book', the problem being that an e-book can be anything from an exact digital copy (or an image) of a printed book comprising essentially the same structure as its physical version, to a complex digital object which takes advantage of all that the online digital domain can offer. This means that searching and functionalities for e-books can vary widely. Searching can be flexible and include Boolean logic and fuzzy searching as provided, for example in the Academic Library collections of e-books.

Oxford Scholarship Online is an example of a collection of multidisciplinary monographs which has full text search. It also offers abstracts (a feature borrowed from journal format) and live links to related references. Other useful features include highlighting search terms and a navigation panel which allows easy navigation around the chapters. An example of a different model is EEBO (Early English Books Online), a collection of images of books, which enables users to 'see' the original pages of these historic texts. Features have been added via the Text Creation Partnership which means that full text and other searches are possible. Knovel is an example of a publisher including not only the text of a publication, but auxiliary information such as databases and spreadsheets. The Knovel Library is a collection of books with related additional data provided and able to be downloaded and manipulated.

The concept of a page sometimes becomes irrelevant in the digital domain, particularly for born-digital items. However, if the book (or journal for that matter) requires some relationship to the print version, for example for citation purposes, the online version will probably retain this physically specific architecture or will provide an indication of the structure of the printed version by, say, including the page number at the start of a new page. Navigation around long texts can be aided by use of navigation windows that might incorporate, say, chapter and section headings with the ability to expand and collapse lists, jumping to the next use of the search term(s), and the means of skipping between pages. A search function allows for controlled searching across the text. Resources such as NetLibrary or eBrary might include features such a notes facility to enable the logged in reader to 'jot down' personal notes, an inbuilt dictionary for defining terms or a highlighter for marking selected text. There might be advanced search features and comprehensive data such as subject headings allowing for precise and flexible searching.

e-Books are often either provided by the publisher themselves or by an aggregator that includes books from many publishers. e-Books can be made available as part of book series such as those that form part of Science Direct from Elsevier. Science Direct also includes encyclopedias as one of its reference works. Although many e-book collections or series are only available to subscribers, there are some notable examples of freely available e-books including Project Gutenberg which comprises out of copyright books and other publications. Another noteable source of e-books is Google where a vast quantity of books are being digitized and access to all or some of the full text is being provided.

Although a reader may prefer not to read large quantities of text, particularly in the case of a novel, on a screen, an electronic version of a novel can have huge benefits for the researcher wishing to analyse texts and search for terms within that text. So far libraries have generally preferred online versions of e-books rather than some of the other platforms available.

Catalogues and bibliographies

The RSLG (Research Support Libraries Group) report of a review of higher education libraries states that 'the OPAC is the most popular discovery tool for researchers overall' (RSLG 2003: para. 64). Catalogues, either libraries' or publishers', are a means of discovering items. Searching the home library catalogue is advantageous because access to items will be easy. For broader coverage or when searching for highly specialist items, use of union catalogues such as COPAC or the British Library will be necessary.

Book publishers should have the most up to date information regarding their own products but the drawback is being forced to check many separate catalogues. They do not include information on out of print titles. Publishers' catalogues are often available both in print and online.

Some publishers focus on particular subject areas and researchers become familiar with the names associated with their own subject.

Most major disciplines have a bibliography that covers the subject. If printed, they will not necessarily be particularly current, but can be of great use for discovering previously published works. The BNB (British National Bibliography) covers all disciplines, including forthcoming titles and is regularly updated: monthly on CD-ROM and weekly in print.

Online bookshops can be used as online catalogues for the discovery of resources.

Research libraries

For the purposes of this chapter, the term, 'research library' can be defined as a large library with an extensive collection of national interest that supports researchers in one or more disciplines and which might act as an archive.

UK national libraries

The UK national libraries are the British Library and the national libraries of Scotland and Wales. National libraries maintain collections of all national printed (and more recently, electronic) publications issued in their own country. This is achieved by a system of legal deposit where either the publishers are obliged to provide the library with a copy of every item they publish, or the library is entitled to request a copy of every item published (see Chapter 2). All provide online catalogues which can be freely searched. The national library might also issue a national bibliography of printed publications, such as the BNB in the UK.

Additionally there are other specialist national libraries in the UK which include:

- The National Art Library at the Victoria and Albert Museum[4]
- The National Electronic Library for Health[5] (NHS – National Health Service)
- The National Electronic Library for Mental Health[6] (NHS)
- BFI (British Film Institute) National Library[7]

Non-UK national libraries

The Library of Congress in the US retains vast holdings and provides online catalogues for searching its extensive collections. The catalogue allows expert search techniques for better retrieval.

The European Library

> is a portal which offers access to the combined resources (books, magazines, journals . . . both digital and non-digital) of the 45 national libraries of Europe. It offers free searching and delivers digital objects – some free, some priced.
>
> (The European Library 2007)

with information about the National libraries of Europe and their online services.

Other countries' national libraries online catalogues are freely available on the WWW. Links to many catalogues may be found via the British Library's website or on one of the Library of Congress Internet resource pages. The British Library is one of the partners in the MACS Project (Multilingual ACcess to Subjects) sponsored by the Conference of European National Librarians (CENL). The other partners are:

- Swiss National Library (SNL)
- Bibliothèque nationale de France (BnF)
- Die Deutsche Bibliothek (DDB)

The project is developing a means of achieving multilingual, multisite searching across national libraries in Europe. Users will be able to search the catalogues of the project's partner libraries simultaneously in the language of their choice (English, French, German).

University research libraries

Although all university libraries tailor their collections to support the research within their own institutions, some retain extensive collections that will be of interest to researchers at a national level. Of the six legal deposit libraries in the UK and Ireland, three are university libraries:

- Bodleian Library, Oxford
- University Library, Cambridge
- Trinity College Library, Dublin

These collections are searchable via OPACs.

The John Rylands University Library of Manchester (JRULM) is the largest academic library in the UK which is not a legal deposit library. It has broad subject coverage and some special collections.

Other university libraries hold extensive and specialist collections in selected subject areas. For example:

- The social sciences collection at the British Library of Political and Economic Science (LSE)
- The legal collection at the IALS[8]

Specialist research libraries

Researchers in specialist subject areas are often able to locate resources in specialist libraries. These may be the libraries of professional bodies, charitable organizations, or centres of research excellence that are not educational institutions, for example, museums. The *ASLIB Directory of Information Sources in the United Kingdom* (Reynard 2004) includes entries for many of these libraries (see above).

Some specialist libraries in main subject areas, all of which have OPACs, are as follows.

Art and humanities:

- British Library Digital Catalogue of Illuminated Manuscripts (DigCIM)
- The Courtauld Institute of Art[9]
- The London Library collection of books in all European languages in the humanities

Engineering and mathematics:

- Institution of Electrical Engineers[10]
- RIBA (Royal Institute of British Architects) British Architectural Library[11]
- London Mathematical Society[12]

Health and life sciences:

- The Wellcome Library for the History and Understanding of Medicine
- Natural History Museum Library[13]
- Royal Horticultural Society[14]
- National Oceanographic Library, Southampton[15]
- Centre for Ecology and Hydrology[16]

Physical sciences:

- The Royal Society of Chemistry[17]
- The Royal Society[18]

Social sciences:

- The Women's library[19]
- London Business School[20]

Research Libraries Group (RLG)

The Research Libraries Group comprises around 160 institutions including universities, national libraries, archives, museums, independent research collections, historical societies, and others. All retain and manage extensive research collections. Members are from all over the world. The group provides a union catalogue for subscribers, but there is free access to the web pages of member institutions.

What's in London's Libraries (WiLL)

The London Libraries Development Agency is working to develop a means of cross-searching public library catalogues and community information databases in 33 London boroughs from any networked terminal in London public libraries (a project funded by the People's Network Excellence Fund). The resulting system, named WiLL,[21] includes some museum and archive databases.

Public libraries

Public library collections are usually of limited use to those undertaking large scale research projects. However, they can be valuable in areas such as local history. Many have OPACs covering the county or area libraries.

Open access materials

Open access journal publishers and suppliers are growing and of increasing importance to the researcher (see Chapter 10). OAIster[22] provides a search interface that enables searching across open access repositories (although results are not limited exclusively to open access materials). More services such as this are expected in the future and a UK institutional **repository** search service is in development.

Other sources and types of information

Databases that contain records of other formats, such as audio visual materials, can be searched in similar ways to bibliographic databases. For example, the British Universities Film and Video Council (BUFVC)[23] provides access to Hermes database of audio visual programmes and the British Universities Newsreel Database (BUND), and the Education Image Gallery (EIG)[24] holds around 50,000 images for use in education. The COPAC union catalogue has a map search option which limits the search to items such as maps, nautical charts, atlases, and topographical drawings.

Grey literature (see Appendix 2) can be difficult to track down. One source for searching US grey literature is the GrayLIT Network, 'a portal for technical report information generated through federally funded research and development projects' (Office of Scientific and Technical Information 2007). Content comprises scientific technical reports. The British Library collection includes UK reports, conferences, and theses. As more **digital repositories** are created and filled, grey literature is likely to become more readily available, but comprehensive coverage will be some time in coming.

ZETOC,[25] the database created jointly by the British Library and the JISC, contains bibliographic details of many thousands of conference proceedings and journals' tables of contents from all disciplines. It is available free to UK further and higher education institutions.

New York Public Library catalogue[26] can be of great use for checking biblio-graphic details of US titles (in addition to the Library of Congress catalogue). It also includes audio visual materials, maps, and artefacts as well as access to the New York Public Library for the Performing Arts dance collection catalogue and the Schomburg Center for Research In Black Culture catalogue.

The BOPCRIS (British Official Publications Collaborative Reader Informa-tion Service)[27] catalogue can be used to discover British Official publications published between 1688 and 1995. Abstracts are provided for many records. The UK National Archives[28] provides access to a central catalogue of govern-ment records and information about UK archives and other collections. UKOP (UK Official Publications), from TSO, is 'the official catalogue of UK official publications since 1980, containing 450,000 records from over 2000 public bodies' (TSO 2007).

Online book sellers such as Amazon are providing increasingly sophisticated services for users. For example, Amazon now includes a facility for publishers to allow the full text of their books to be searched and for sections to be made freely accessible as a 'taster' for users. If available, this can be useful for researchers who are trying to ascertain whether or not a title is relevant to them.

References and citation searching

Scrutinizing the references included in works and performing a citation search (see Chapter 7) are valuable methods of discovering information.

Selecting sources relevant to the subject

Searchers often develop tunnel vision when it comes to using databases. They know and use one or two databases, which cover their chosen subject, and ignore others. It is true that there is usually a large, reliable, and well known database for most broad subject areas, but that does not mean it is the only resource. Neither does it mean that other more general databases do not cover the subject. For example, subscribers can access the British Library Inside data-base to search for research articles and conference proceedings in all subject disciplines.

Researchers should familiarize themselves with the range of databases avail-able to them, including general titles. For example, Science Direct from the publisher Elsevier does not imply from its title that it will be of any use to researchers in subjects other than pure science. In fact, the subject coverage includes journal titles in the fields of:

• Arts and humanities

- Business, management, and accounting
- Economics, econometrics, and finance

Checking the content and coverage of databases (see above) is imperative for running a comprehensive search or finding an item not listed in the chosen favoured database.

Key points

- Information discovery is the process of finding details of relevant information
- Researchers need to find the details, bibliographic or otherwise, of items that are required
- Online bibliographic databases are a means of finding bibliographic details of items
- Searchers should check the facilities and help function of each database
- Records that have been discovered and searches and search histories can be saved for future reference
- Catalogues, bibliographies, and lists of references can be used to discover items
- Researchers should use a variety of databases for comprehensive searching and beware database tunnel vision

---

Checklist

1   Which databases, abstracts and indexes are most relevant to your research? Are there other more general databases which will also be useful?
2   Is there a federated search option at your institutional library (where you can search across a number of databases at one go)?
3   Select a key database for your research and find out about the fields it indexes, whether or not it has a thesaurus, if there is useful information on the help function, and how you can manage the records you retrieve (marking, emailing, using bibliographic software). Are there any quirks that you should know about?
4   Do you know how to find open access journals and other open access materials?
5   Which national library catalogues and collections and specialist research collections should you check?
6   Which sources of information about other types of materials will you use (e.g., archives, official documents, grey literature, images, or maps)?

6

The online searching process

The importance of planning a search • The online searching process • How to plan a search strategy • When to run the search • Evaluating the results • Saving the results • Completion of the search

The importance of planning a search

Someone running a search on a database or search engine might sit at the computer, access a favourite database/search engine, type in a word and see what happens, with little or no prior thought given to the method of searching. The consequence of this unplanned searching is that the searcher may stumble across some relevant references fairly quickly – or not. There may be innumerable hits, or very few, and what is retrieved may be irrelevant. Faced with this unsatisfactory result, the searcher will then enter an alternative search term which may produce similarly unsuccessful results to the first. This process may be repeated until either the searcher has gathered what they think is a reasonable list of records for the task in hand, or until they become so frustrated that they give up.

Any suitable references resulting from this type of search are a result of luck rather than planning and, most importantly, the searcher may have missed key references. It could result in a piece of work presented with a large number of references, most of which are peripheral to the subject and omitting work by well known specialists in the field of study.

Those undertaking any type of research need to find information efficiently. In the first instance of planning the research project, it is vital that researchers are fully aware of the work of others so that time is not wasted and work is not repeated unwittingly: expert searching skills will aid this process. When undertaking research for papers or books that are to be published or sent for peer review, it is important that references to relevant publications are not omitted and that the author demonstrates a complete knowledge of the current situation in their chosen field.

Sadly the poor searching scenario such as the one above happens all too frequently. Kate Hodgson of CMS Cameron McKenna wrote of the searching techniques of legal trainees:

> Most trainees use such poor search strategies and techniques on both the web and commercial databases. Over 80% of searches carried out are for one single word. The concepts searched for are not thought-out, the key terms are not identified, relationships between key terms are not thought through, and Boolean logic might as well be a clue in a Vulcan crossword.
>
> (Hodgson 2002: 14)

Poor search techniques are not only used by legal trainees. The JUSTEIS (JISC Usage Surveys: Trends in Electronic Information Services) project investigated the behaviour of end users of electronic information services. One finding was that 'postgraduates may be focused and persistent in their searching [of search engines] but do not necessarily employ cohesive strategies' (Armstrong et al. 2000: sect. 6.3.3). The user behaviour section concludes that 'given the wide range of engines used and the haphazard nature of much of the searching, some thought might be given to ways of encouraging students to use the Internet more effectively'. These findings are applicable to search techniques using structured databases. Single word searching *can* be useful when using specific specialist terms or as part of a more complex search strategy where terms will be combined later, but searchers should not rely solely on this technique. In cases where the single search term is broad (for example, 'sociology' or 'perception'), the numbers of hits may be extremely high and therefore unmanageable.

Having explained the problems associated with poor search techniques resulting from a lack of a systematic approach, the benefits of planning a search strategy should be noted.

Planning a search strategy:

- Results in the retrieval of relevant references
- Avoids omitting key references
- Is more likely to retrieve a manageable number of results
- Uses time efficiently

Searching using successful techniques can be time consuming. It is, however, far preferable to spend the time profitably, retrieving relevant results rather than wasting precious time gathering poor results.

The online searching process

The searching process is both iterative and heuristic. It is a circular rather than a linear process. It can best be defined as being complete when the searcher retrieves records that they have already identified as of use and no new relevant records are thrown up. In some ways, the search can never be described as complete owing to the fact that additional terms and new information will be encountered as the research progresses.

The search process comprises the following steps:

- PLAN: IDENTIFY the terms and FORMULATE the search strategy
- RUN the search
- RETRIEVE relevant results
- EVALUATE the results
- SAVE relevant results
- MODIFY and re-run the search

all the time keeping records of the process (see Figure 6.1).

What follows is a description of the process when searching online, but many of the techniques are also relevant when searching using print sources

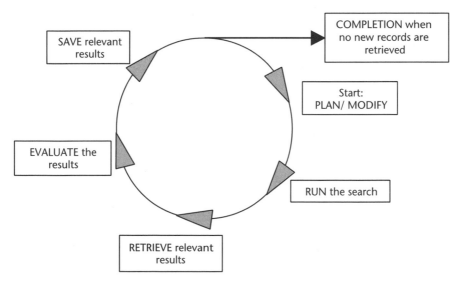

Figure 6.1 The online search process

How to plan a search strategy

Tempting though it is to begin using large and powerful databases straight away, the following method is recommended prior to the search.

The practical method of planning a search strategy depends on the preferences of the individual. Some will opt for paper and pencil, others may use a word processor, and some will draw spider diagrams or similar (for example, see Tony Buzan's detailed books, including *Mind Mapping: Kickstart Your Creativity and Transform Your Life* (Buzan 2006)) perhaps with the aid of specialist software.

The researcher should plan the next five steps before proceeding with the search.

1 Identify search terms
2 Limit the search
3 Truncation, wildcards, and phrases
4 Combining terms 1 (Boolean logic)
5 Combining terms 2 (using other connectors)

See Figure 6.2 for a diagrammatic representation of these steps.

Step 1: Identify search terms

The area of research and the information need will already have been defined (see Chapters 1 and 4). Using what has been defined, the next step is to focus on the words that will be used to find information. The terms which are selected for searching are the foundation from which the research grows.

When reading around the subject in the initial stages of the work, keep a record of significant words which may later be used for searching. Together with the formal designation of concepts and search terms, these words can be used to build up a matrix of keywords for the execution of the search.

It is beneficial to have a dictionary, a thesaurus, and, possibly, encyclopaedias to hand, including any specialist subject publications such as a dictionary of the subject area (for example, a dictionary of economics). Research supervisors and other specialists can offer help with the selection of search terms.

For example, the hypothesis might be:

> The news media in the UK is more concerned with sensationalism than balanced reporting.

The main topics can be broken down into sub-topics and linked areas which will also suggest possible search terms. To achieve this the researcher might:

1 Create a list using main and sub-headings

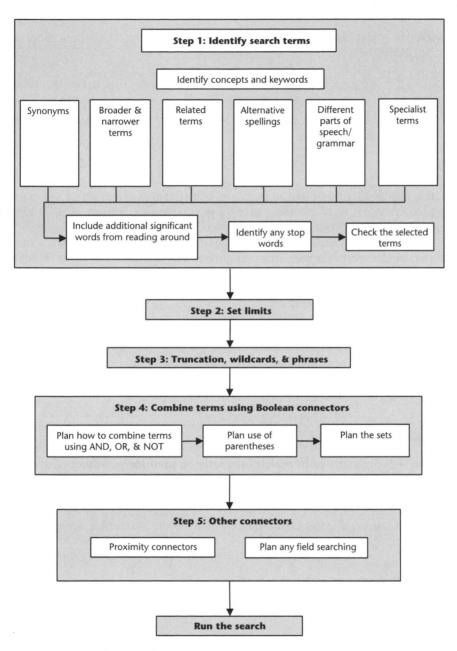

Figure 6.2 The five search steps

2 Compile a table or
3 Draw a spider diagram or similar (the choice depending on the preference of the researcher)

Figures 6.3, 6.4, and 6.5 show representations of topics as headings and subheadings, a table and a spider diagram (which can be hand drawn) respectively. They are by no means exhaustive, but give an outline of a possible solution.

Concepts

Using the title (or statement or question) as a starting point, extract the main concepts (topics or ideas) and list them in a table or use them as a starting point for a spider diagram.

It is advisable to limit the number of concepts to a maximum of four. Any more, and the search becomes over-complex. A large number of concepts may indicate that the area of research has not been succinctly defined or is too broad.

Example title:

> With reference to organizations in the UK, to what extent has the 'glass ceiling' been shattered?

Figure 6.6 shows an example of the concepts using a table. The topics from above can be included in the plans.

Synonyms

The researcher's title or hypothesis may use one particular word, but articles written on the same topic may include a similar one instead. The effect of not including synonyms in the search is that the records retrieved will exclude relevant material that doesn't happen to use identical words.

The concept term 'organization' in the example above has a number of synonyms, including:

- company
- corporation
- federation
- firm
- institution

Use of a thesaurus will make the task of identifying synonyms easier. Structured databases often include a thesaurus which the researcher should consider using.

The news media in the UK is more concerned with sensationalism than balanced reporting

1 News media

1.1 Individual characteristics of selected publications:
Reporting styles
Use of language
Use of images and other audio visual devices
Readership/viewing or listening profiles
The coverage of different subject areas (for example, politics, human interest, environment)

1.2 Types of news media in the UK:
Newspapers (broadsheet and tabloid)
Television (public service and commercial; land, cable, and satellite)
Radio (public service and commercial)
Internet news

1.3 The people involved:
Reporters
Editors
Newspaper owners
Readers
Subjects of the stories and so on

2 Sensationalism

2.1 Define sensationalism:
Dictionary definition
Definition used in these investigations

2.2 Attitudes towards sensationalism in the UK:
Attitudes of the general populace

2.3 The law in the UK:
Privacy laws
Libel and slander

3 Balanced reporting

3.1 Define balanced reporting:
Dictionary definition
Definition used in these investigations

3.2 Commercial interests:
Vested interests
Viewing/listening/readership figures

3.3 Impartiality

Figure 6.3 Topics shown as main headings and sub-headings

Main title:
'The news media in the UK is more concerned with sensationalism than balanced reporting'

	Concept 1 News media			Concept 2 Sensationalism			Concept 3 Balanced reporting		
	Topic area 1 Individual characteristics of selected publications	**Topic area 2** Types of news media in the UK	**Topic area 3** The people involved	**Topic area 1** Define sensationalism	**Topic area 2** Attitudes towards sensationalism in the UK	**Topic area 3** The Law in the UK	**Topic area 1** Define balanced reporting	**Topic area 2** Commercial interests	**Topic area 3** Impartiality
Reporting styles		Newspapers (broadsheet and tabloid)	Reporters	Dictionary definition	Attitudes of the general populace	Privacy laws Libel and slander	Dictionary definition	Vested interests	
Use of language		Television (public service and commercial, land, cable, and satellite)	Editors	Definition used in these investigations			Definition used in these investigations	Viewing/ listening/ readership figures	
Use of images and other audio visual devices		Radio (public service and commercial) Internet news	Newspaper owners						
Readership/ viewing or listening profiles			Readers						
The coverage of different subject areas (for example, politics, human interest, environment)			Subjects of the stories and so on						

Figure 6.4 Topics shown in table format

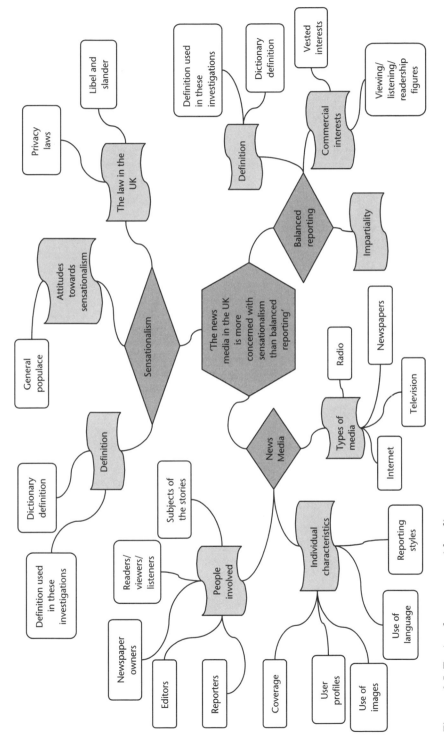

Figure 6.5 Topics shown as a spider diagram

With reference to organizations in the UK, to what extent has the 'glass ceiling' been shattered?			
CONCEPTS	Glass ceiling	Organizations	UK
SYNONYMS			
BROADER TERMS			
NARROWER TERMS			
RELATED TERMS			
ALTERNATIVE SPELLINGS			
PARTS OF SPEECH			

Figure 6.6 Example of concepts shown as a table

Include both the abbreviation and the full words in the search strategy. For example:

- UK   United Kingdom
- EOC   Equal Opportunities Commission
- kHz   kilohertz

Figures present a similar case. Include amounts in both figures and words when dealing with situations such as dates:

- 1930s   nineteen thirties
- 14th century   fourteenth century

Hyphens can present a problem, so err on the side of caution and include both forms, with and without the hyphen if appropriate. For example:

- neoclassical   neo-classical

Always check the help function of the database for guidance.

An area of which to be aware is where a change of name has taken place, for example:

- Department for Education
- Department of Education and Science (DES)
- Department for Education and Skills (DfES)

Go through each search term carefully, identifying the relevant synonyms, and include them in the table or diagram. Table 6.1 demonstrates how many records might be missed if synonyms are not used.

Table 6.1 Search using synonyms for the term 'organizations'

Term/synonym	Numbers of records retrieved
Organizations	6501
Firms	5603
Companies	2761
Institutions	7648
Corporations	1800

Source: Searches run on *IBSS* (advanced search: title field), 21.1.07

When checking the databases' thesauri, the searcher may encounter the instruction, 'Use for . . .' This occurs when the indexer has selected a particular term instead of one or more other possibilities. For example, one might encounter:

- Workers: *Use for* employee/employees

In this case, the query should not include the term 'employees', but substitute the term 'workers'.

Broader and narrower terms

For each concept, broader and narrower terms should be considered as possibilities for inclusion in the search. One can think of broader and narrower terms using the analogy of a man. Progressively broader terms could be:

- Human being
- Mammal
- Vertebrate

and so on. Progressively narrower terms could be:

- Human blood circulatory system
- Human blood
- Human red blood cells

and so on.

It can be helpful to think of viewing terms through both a telescope for a broader view and a microscope for the detail. The result is a hierarchy of terms. One can think of keywords as part of a hierarchy with broader terms above and more specific, narrower terms below (see Figure 6.7).

The researcher should use their judgement to decide which terms are relevant to their search and therefore included. Databases sometimes use an 'Explode' function to list narrower terms. This can be a helpful method of drilling down to the most relevant search terms, ignoring irrelevant terms.

The use of broader and narrower terms depends on the individual piece of work. For example, a researcher may decide that it is necessary to include narrower terms in the search strategy, but not broader terms. Be aware though, of the types of results that this action might exclude (see Boolean NOT searching

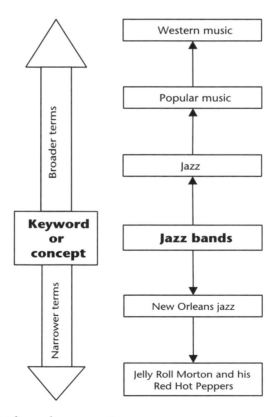

Figure 6.7 Broader and narrower terms

below). The reasons for inclusion/exclusion of broader and/or narrower terms may include:

- The numbers of retrieved records are too many/too few
- The concept is such a specialist or specific term as to be the most narrow available
- A broader term would be so broad as to be irrelevant
- The searcher would like an overview of the general situation in order to place the chosen topic in context
- Examples in specific areas are required
- An example of an identical test situation is required therefore broader or narrower terms are irrelevant

Related terms

A related term is one which is linked to the search terms by subject matter, but which may not be included in the synonyms or broader or narrower terms. In the example, terms related to 'glass ceiling' might be:

- promotion
- personnel management
- discrimination
- women

Subject knowledge and experience should be used to select related terms to be included in the search. Some databases include a function to retrieve records that have been indexed as related records to those already retrieved (see Chapter 5). See also the section on evaluation of the results below. If a database includes a thesaurus, related terms may be included.

Alternative spellings

Many words have alternative spellings, especially British/US spellings, and it is important to be aware of them. If the search is run using a single spelling option, the database may not automatically retrieve records with alternative(s), leaving the results incomplete and the searcher unaware that they have missed potentially large numbers of records. Table 6.2 demonstrates this point. Common variants in spelling are shown in Table 6.3.

Databases vary in their ability to recognize and incorporate alternative spellings. It is safer to assume that it will not automatically incorporate any alternatives. Find out about the individual database's capability by checking the 'Help' function of the database, or scan the results to see whether or not they are included.

At this point in the planning process, check the broader, narrower, and related terms selected for synonyms and alternative spellings.

Table 6.2 Example of searches using alternative spellings

	Search term	Numbers of records retrieved
Search 1	Behaviour	27,732
Search 2	Behavior	453,631
Difference between searches 1 and 2		425,899

Source: Search run on the APA PsychINFO database without limits selected, 21.01.07

Table 6.3 Common variants in spelling

	Common spelling variants	Example
UK and US English	our/or s/z double letters re/er difference in word	Humour/humor organisation/organization woollen/woolen centre/center speciality/specialty
Archaic words		matins/mattins
Words with Latin/Greek root	Ligatures	encyclopædia/fœtus encyclopaedia/foetus encyclopedia/fetus
New accepted simplified spelling		sulphur/sulfur
Foreign words	ö/oe	Schröder/Schroeder poppadom/poppadam
Colloquialisms/slang		pukka/pukkah/pucca

Different parts of speech/grammar

Not only should plurals of nouns be included where appropriate, but also different parts of speech.

Some databases will include plurals automatically when running a search. Others will include common plurals such as the addition of a letter 's' or 'es' but check whether or not more complex plurals are automatically included. These may include words such as:

- party/parties
- thesaurus/thesauri
- criterion/criteria

There are cases when one should consider all forms of the words in addition to the plural. This can include noun, verb, adjective, past tense, and so on. In the example above the searcher may choose to use some or all of the following:

- organisation
- organisational
- organisationally

not forgetting to include the alternative s/z spelling. In this case 'organise' and 'organised' can probably be ignored.

Phrase or separate words

When referring to searching queries, a phrase can be defined as two or more words that are required consecutively and in a given order for example, 'League of Nations' or 'chicken pox'.

When a phrase occurs among the search terms, the searcher must decide whether or not they want to search for those words as a phrase, or split the words and search for them either individually or in a different word order. This will create quite different searches.

One would probably choose not to split the phrase in the example above. 'Glass ceiling' has a specific meaning and the words are unlikely to be used in a different form (although there is the possibility that the record may contain the same words used differently, but with the same meaning for example, 'ceiling of glass'). 'European Court of Human Rights' is another example of a phrase with a specific meaning that should remain intact when searching. Whereas a searcher faced with the phrase 'juvenile crime' is likely to consider using the words 'juvenile' and 'crime' separately.

Specialist terms

Use of specialist terms will often narrow a search down and produce particularly relevant records if the term appears in the title, abstract, or indexing terms. This can create difficulties if the term is relatively new and few records include it. Alternatively, use of a specialist term can help reduce the numbers of results when too many are being retrieved. There is often no alternative for a specialist term, for example, 'Stroop test' is a particular type of test familiar to psychologists for which there is no obvious alternative.

Checking the terms selected

Having worked through the steps above to arrive at a selection of search terms, the searcher should check the completed table or spider diagram carefully for omissions. Figure 6.8 is by no means exhaustive, but should give an impression of how the finished table may appear.

With reference to organizations in the UK, to what extent has the 'glass ceiling' been shattered?			
CONCEPTS	**Glass ceiling**	**Organizations**	**UK**
SYNONYMS		firms	United Kingdom
		companies	
		institutions	
		corporations	
		enterprises	
BROADER TERMS			Western Europe
			Europe
NARROWER TERMS		SMEs	Great Britain
		small and medium enterprises	Britain
		plc	Northern Ireland
		public limited company	Scotland
			Wales
			England
RELATED TERMS	promotion	businesses	
	personnel management	workplace	
	discrimination	offices	
	equal opportunities	management structure	
	Equal Opportunites Commission		
	women		
	female		
ALTERNATIVE SPELLINGS	EOC	organizations	
PARTS OF SPEECH	promoted	organization	British
	discriminatory	institutional	Scottish
	discriminate	corporate	
	woman	corporation	
	females		
	sex discrimination		
	gender discrimination		

Figure 6.8 Completed table of search terms

Noise or stop words

Databases are usually designed not to accept searches that include common words such as 'by,' 'but', 'if', and so on. Other words that may not be accepted are those that can be used as a command, for example 'within' or 'near' (see below). These disallowed words are called stop (or noise) words. The database may display a message informing the user that a disallowed word has been included or that too many records will be retrieved. Check whether stop words may be included perhaps by the addition of quotation marks: they are usually allowed if they form part of a phrase, for example

- 'Near miss'
- 'Trial by jury'

Step 2: Limiting the search

In addition to defining what is required from the search, it is equally import-ant to define what is not required and how the search may be limited. The scope of the search will already have been decided (see Chapter 4).

Databases vary in the limiting options they offer and each should be checked to see what is available. Take advantage of the limiting options as they will enable the search to be more specific and the results more relevant.

Common limiting options include:

- Language: there is little point in retrieving results in a language that is incomprehensible to the researcher (unless translating facilities are avail-able) and many databases index items in foreign languages. Check the lan-guage of the document, as the database record may be in say, English, but the full text of the item in a different language.
- Date of publication: researchers may wish to retrieve records from a particu-lar period for example, only the most recent publications.
- Type of publication: in addition to references to journal articles, many data-bases contain references to items such as book reviews, dissertation abstracts, audio cassettes, reports, and books.

Databases vary in the limit options they offer: some can be sparse while others contain many options. For example, the Compendex database quick search offers limiting options of:

- document type
- treatment type (that is, the viewpoint of the document)
- language
- date of publication

PsycINFO has a comprehensive selection of limits including:

- language
- publication type
- publication year
- methodology
- age group
- audience type
- document type
- population

Step 3: Truncation, wildcards, and phrases

Truncation

Truncation is sometimes referred to as stemming or root expansion. The words which are identified as search terms when considering different parts of speech often have the beginning of the word (or stem) in common. For example:

- organization
- organizations
- organizational

all have the same *organizatio* . . . as the start of the word.

A specified symbol can take the place of the remainder of the word. This enables a search for a number of words using a single query, therefore saving time and the search becoming unmanageably complex.

The truncated search term may be:

- organizatio*
- organizatio?
- organizatio$

or other variations.

The symbols used for truncation vary, so check which symbol to use for each database. Using the incorrect symbol will result in unreliable results or no results.

Before searching using a truncated term check it will not result in unintended references. For example:

- philan*

will not only retrieve philanthrope, philanthropic, philanthropine, philanthropism, philanthropist but also philanderer!

Use a dictionary to help select and check truncation possibilities.

Problems may arise when searching using truncation on short words, for example, when searching for the singular and plural of the word pit:

- pit?

In this case use of the truncation symbol will retrieve many unwanted terms including pitch; pitted; pithy; pitchfork; pituitary. If the searcher only requires the plural form of this word, it would be better to use an OR search (see below) or a single wildcard symbol (if it can take the place of no character as well as one character).

- pit OR pits
- pit*

Note that use of the wildcard will also retrieve 'pith'.

Wildcards

A wildcard (or universal character) is a symbol that can be used in place of one character, no character, or sometimes a group of characters. They may be incorporated within or at the end of a word. Wildcards are not usually permitted at the start of words. Like truncation symbols, databases vary and the 'Help' function should be checked to find which symbol should be used, and how it should be incorporated. In the following examples, the symbol? has been used as the wildcard.

Single character wildcards can be used to replace one character at a time only. For example, when searching for words such as woman and women:

- wom?n

More than one wildcard may be used, each representing one character, for example:

- bacterioly???

will retrieve bacteriolysis and bacteriolytic.

Depending on the database, the wildcard may also represent no character, useful when searching for alternative spellings. For example:

- behavio?r

will retrieve both the British and US versions of this word. It may also be used at the end of a word, for example, for retrieving singular and plurals:

- trustee?

Some databases allow the use of multicharacter wildcards. These can take the place of a group of characters and can be used for alternative spellings, for example:

- encyclop?dia

will retrieve all spellings of the word.

Phrases

Phrases can make the retrieved results more relevant as there are more criteria for the search. When using a phrase with which to search, some databases require double inverted commas, for example:

- "glass ceiling"

The searcher should be aware of the default of the database they are using. For some, two or more words as the search query will automatically result in a phrase search, others default to an AND or an OR search, which will produce quite different results (see below).

Step 4: Combining terms 1 (Boolean logic)

Being able to combine search terms in a meaningful way allows the searcher to be specific about what they wish to retrieve from the database. When executed properly, this means that the results should contain relevant records and ignore others.

Boolean logic is named after the English mathematician George Boole (d. 1864) who developed a method of notation for logic statements. There are three Boolean connectors (or operators) that can be used between the search terms.

- AND
- OR
- NOT

As with truncation and wildcards, each database should be checked for the actual operators as they vary (for example, some use AND NOT or BUT NOT instead of NOT). Use of these connectors can be most clearly represented using Venn diagrams. Each circle represents the records containing the given term.

AND

Combining two (or more) terms with the AND connector means that the results must contain both (or all) of the words. This means records that include fewer than all of the terms will be ignored.

Using an AND search will narrow down the number of results. Figure 6.9 demonstrates the search query: university AND funding. The hatched area where the circles overlap represents the records that will be retrieved. The remainder will be ignored.

Adding more terms using AND narrows the results further. Figure 6.10 shows the effect of adding another term (UK) to the previous query: the area where the three circles overlap in the centre representing the records retrieved has shrunk in size from that in Figure 6.9.

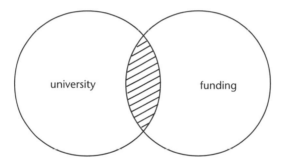

Figure 6.9 Search query: university AND funding

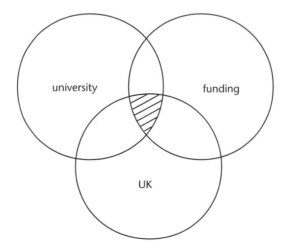

Figure 6.10 Search query: university AND funding AND UK

Some databases will allow the use of a symbol such as & or + instead of typing AND.

OR

The OR connector is generally used when there are two or more alternative terms and the searcher requires that records containing both (or all) are included in the search. Consequently, an OR connector broadens the search. Figure 6.11 shows a basic OR search.

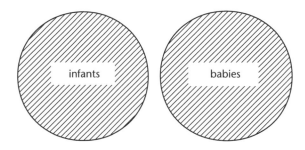

Figure 6.11 Search query: infants OR babies

NOT

The NOT connector is used when a particular term is to be excluded from the search. This may be either to limit the search or to clarify meaning. For example, for articles about continental Europe only, and not including the UK

- Europe NOT UK

An example of clarifying meaning could be:

- macintosh NOT computer

and other homographs:

- ash NOT tree

Figure 6.12 shows the effect of the search query Europe NOT UK. In this example, records including the word 'Europe' will be retrieved, but if there is a single instance of the word 'UK' it will be ignored. This is a useful means of disregarding irrelevant records, but the area of overlap where both terms appear will not be retrieved.

The searcher should use their skill and judgement when dealing with

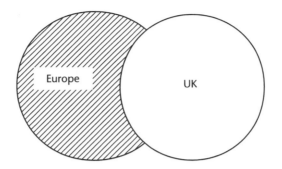

Figure 6.12 Search query: Europe NOT UK

homographs as to which word(s) to exclude. Evaluation of the results will aid the decision (see below).

Some databases will allow the use of a symbol such as % instead of typing NOT.

Implied Boolean logic

Another search option that the searcher may encounter is that of Boolean logic that has been disguised to make the search page more user friendly.

Find results:

- With all the words: equates to an AND search
- With some of the terms/with at least one of the words: equates to an OR search
- Without the terms/excluding these words: equates to a NOT search
- With the exact phrase: is a phrase search

Additionally, search within the results performs an AND search.

Parentheses

When combining terms it is easy unintentionally to create a search strategy that is ambiguous. In order to avoid this many databases allow the use of parentheses.

The 'Help' function may give the order in which the search commands are prioritized. Parentheses are usually considered first. Check this information on the database(s) being used. The need for parentheses can be demonstrated by a simple mathematical problem:

(a) $6\,(4+5)$
(b) $6 \times 4 + 5$
(c) $6 \times 4 + 6 \times 5$

The answer to (a) is 54. To calculate this correctly the solver *must* first solve the parentheses either by solving the sum in parentheses or multiplying each number in the parentheses by 6.

The answer to (b) could be 29 (that is 24 + 5) or 54 (that is 6 x 9) depending on the order which the solver uses. The solution to (c) could be 150 or 54 or 300. (b) and (c) could be corrected by the addition of parentheses:

(b) as (a) or $(6 \times 4) + 5$
(c) $(6 \times 4) + (6 \times 5)$ or $6(4 + 6) \times 5$ and so on

The same rules apply when using parentheses for search queries. For example:

- Women OR female AND "equal opportunities" OR discrimination

If the database deals with AND connectors before OR connectors, the result of this search may be quite unlike what the searcher intended. That is, female AND "equal opportunities" would be solved first.

The addition of parentheses immediately solves the problem of ambiguity:

- (women OR female) AND ("equal opportunities" OR discrimination)

Those parts of the query in parentheses will be dealt with first, followed by the remaining AND instruction. Figure 6.13 demonstrates the different results.

It can be helpful to say the search strings out loud to determine whether or not they are ambiguous.

How to combine terms in practice

Using the table or spider diagram of relevant terms go through them, deciding how best to combine them so that all possibilities are covered. This may mean that a long list of search queries is created. Use of truncation and wildcards will reduce the numbers of queries.

If possible, keep queries relatively simple. This can be for two reasons:

- Long, complex search queries are liable to include errors.
- Use of a larger number of short search queries reduces the margin of error and allows the searcher to be flexible by combining previously run searches in different ways.

For example, using the glass ceiling example above, the searcher may construct the following search strategies:

- "glass ceiling" AND (organi*atio? OR compan? OR institutio?) AND (UK OR "united kingdom")

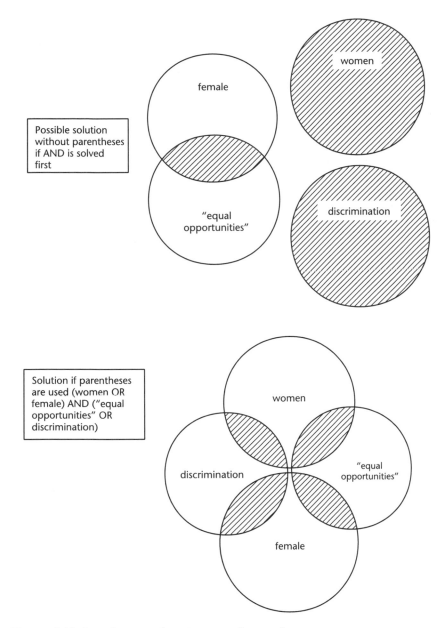

Figure 6.13 Search query showing use of parentheses

- (EOC OR "equal opportunities commission") AND (wom*n OR femal?) AND workplace
- (EOC OR "equal opportunities commission") AND (wom*n OR femal?) AND promot?

[W]here? is used as a truncation symbol and * is used for a single character wildcard. In order to include all the terms they wish, the searcher will have to construct a large number of complex search strings. It would be preferable, to run a larger number of simpler searches that can then be combined later, giving more flexibility. For example:

1 organi*atio? OR compan? OR institutio?
2 UK OR "united kingdom" OR british OR britain OR "great britain"
3 promot?
4 equal opportunit? OR "equal opportunies commission" OR EOC
5 discriminat?
6 wom*n OR femal?

giving sets 1 to 6 and so on. The searcher can then combine searches in as many combinations as is required as shown in Table 6.4.

Table 6.4 Combined searches

Combined searches	Set number
(1) AND (2)	7
(3) AND (4)	8
(5) AND (6)	9
(3) AND (6)	10
set 7 AND set 8 AND set 9	11
(1) AND (5)	12

The resulting sets can be combined until the researcher is content that all appropriate combinations have been included.

Some of these less complex searches may result in very large numbers of results, which at first seem unmanageable. However, when these results are combined with others using an AND connector, the numbers will diminish because use of this operator has the effect of narrowing down the search.

The functions of the database(s) selected will dictate the exact method of combining the searches.

Step 5: Combining terms 2 (using other connectors)

Depending on the database(s) selected, additional connectors may be available. Use of these allows adaptation to focus the search. These devices are called proximity operators or connectors. Details of phrase searching may be included with the instructions for proximity connectors. The options usually comprise one or more of the following:

- Terms within the same sentence or paragraph
- Terms within a specified number of words of each other
- Terms in a specified order (but not necessarily adjacent)

Terms within the same sentence or paragraph

If terms appear within the same sentence or paragraph, there is more likelihood that they have some relevance to each other. This is particularly true when searching the full texts of documents. If an AND search is selected, one term may appear near the beginning of the text and the other, not included until somewhere near the end. To achieve increased relevance, specify documents where the terms are used in close proximity so they are likely to have some relation to each other. To search for terms within the same sentence (in no particular order) use a connector such as /s. For example:

- slang /s french

and for terms within the same paragraph use /p. For example:

- slang /p dialect

Each database should be checked for the methods of doing this.

Terms within a specified number of words of each other

Databases vary in how they require the command for this instruction. The connector will retrieve records with the terms within a specified proximity of each other, but not usually in any particular order. For example:

- bridge within 6 span

or

- bridge /6 span

The records retrieved may include phrases such as:

- The Sydney Harbour Bridge has a span of . . .
- The span of any bridge that is built . . .

Another method of achieving a similar result is using the NEAR connector. As with all other connectors, databases should be checked for the options available and the means of executing them. It is up to the discretion of the searcher to select the number for the proximity of the terms.

Terms in a specified order

The option to specify that terms should be in a particular order (but not necessarily adjacent) may be available. This might be achieved by using the connectors BEFORE or AFTER. For example:

- gin BEFORE tonic
- flu AFTER avian

A variation of this is being able to specify one word preceding another within the same sentence or same paragraph by incorporating operators, for example, +s (for preceding within the same sentence) or +p (for preceding within the same paragraph).

When to run the search

Having selected the relevant database(s) to use (see Chapter 5), it is at this point that the search is run. The search can be planned up to step four then additional connectors used to refine the results. Although it may seem a large amount of work, the planning process will save time and frustration as the searcher can be confident of having covered the most relevant terms and has a record of the process, making any revisions a straightforward procedure.

Evaluating the results

It is vital at every stage of the search that the retrieved records are investigated for relevance. By doing this that the searcher can be sure they are finding the records they require. Criteria for evaluation should include:

- Numbers of records retrieved
- Position and frequency of the keywords used for the search (search terms are usually highlighted within retrieved records)
- Inclusion of homographs, unintended truncated words and other irrelevant results
- Additional relevant terms not included in the search strategy

- Types of document retrieved
- Any factors that may be limited in a future search (for example, date of publication, language)
- Checking for related terms and relevant indexing terms or descriptors
- Level of writing
- Overall relevance of the subject matter to the work being undertaken

Use the information gleaned to modify and improve the search strategy.
Evaluation can take two forms:

1 Quick scanning to check that the results are what was expected
2 Indepth evaluation to identify records that will be saved and later followed up to find the full text

Quick scanning can be used when retrieving large numbers of records. The evaluation will move towards becoming more indepth as the search begins to focus on fewer, more relevant records.

The amount of records that constitute a 'manageable number' is a personal preference.

Saving the results

Once the relevant records have been retrieved, save those which are deemed useful for the project. Not only should the records be saved, but also the search strategy and history so that the search can be re-run and/or the searches, already performed, can be easily checked.

See Chapters 5 and 13 regarding saving searches and records, and managing the results of searches.

Completion of the search

When relevant records that have already been retrieved appear and no new records are being pulled up, the searcher can conclude that, for the present, the search is complete. New records are constantly being added to databases so it is important that during the course of the project, previously run searches are updated. As the research progresses, more terms may be encountered that should be included in search strategies, so new search queries will be devised using these terms.

Key points

- Plan and formulate a search strategy before embarking on a search using a structured database
- Searching is an iterative and heuristic process
- Do not cut corners or leave too little time
- The aim of the search is to retrieve a manageable number of relevant results
- Experience and careful evaluation of the records retrieved will help the improvement of searching techniques

Checklist

1 Having read around the subject, you should now have a record of significant words which may be used for searching
2 Identify the concepts and keywords and work through the steps in Figure 6.2
3 Incorporate Boolean and other connectors as well as devices such as truncation and wildcards to focus the search and retrieve relevant records
4 Set limits on the search or use the NOT connector to ignore extraneous records
5 Do you need to refine, broaden, or narrow your searches?
6 Are the results what you expected?
7 Evaluate the results at each stage using what is found to modify and improve the search strategy
8 Have you saved all the relevant records so that you have all the information necessary for acquiring the full text?
9 Have you got to the point where you are not retrieving new records?
10 Are there any other databases or other sources you should use?

7

Citation searching

*What is citation searching and why is it important? • Citation indexes
• When to stop • Electronic citation searching • Problems associated with
citation searching • Cross-referencing*

What is citation searching and why is it important?

Having obtained a published work to support the research, the genealogy of the
selected work is of importance when researching a topic thoroughly. Citation
searching is similar to creating a family tree in finding who begat whom or, at
least, which work influenced another. It is carried out in tandem with database
and other searches.

Citation searching works on the basis of who cited whom in their work. This
means that it is a case of working backwards and forwards in time to find
where a particular work has been cited:

- Working backwards in time: following up the citations given in the article
- Working forwards in time: finding out where the article has been cited

Figure 7.1 shows how related works link by their references. It also demonstrates the complexity of the task. Imagine how Work 11 is discovered: this
might be achieved by finding the reference made to it in Work 2. A researcher
would not directly find Work 11 by reading the Starting point work. However,
if they read Work 2 which is cited in the Starting point work, they would then
discover Work 11 (dotted line).

Citation searching is a process of finding works that are related, sometimes
closely, by discovering those an author used (and referenced) when writing
their own.

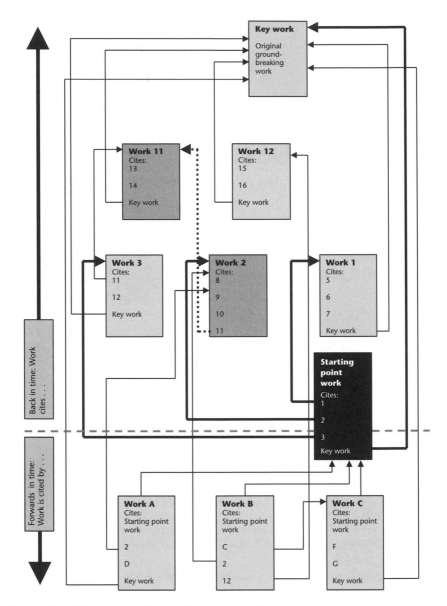

Figure 7.1 The complexity of citation searching

The reasons for performing a citation search

There are many reasons why a researcher may perform a citation search:

• Finding the original work(s) on which an idea or research is based
• Finding reactions to a work
• Finding works that are closely related
• Finding authors working in a similar field
• Following up further developments in that field
• Retrieving information about corrections or retractions of published work
• Mapping trends in research
• Identifying emerging research areas
• Finding the frequency and the publications where works have been cited
• Finding the impact of one author's work on others' work
• Finding the effect of research
• Finding the influence of research on innovation, particularly when searching citations in a patent
• Finding background information in a chosen topic
• When experiencing difficulties in discovering works using subject keyword searching

Lawrence et al. argue that citation indexing also improves communication (Lawrence et al. 1999: 67).

Citation indexes

A citation index is a record of cited references, usually in the form of a published list or an electronic database. For example, the Current Law Case Citator lists all English court cases that have been reported since 1947 as well as subsequent cases which have made reference to the case in question. For those working in other fields, the ISI Web of Knowledge (WoK) databases provides three indexes:

• Arts and humanities citation index
• Science citation index
• Social science citation index

The Elsevier databases, Scopus and Science Direct also have sophisticated citation searching functions and other sources such as OUP's Oxford Journals include some aspects of citation searching. Citation searching features can include:

• Lists of references cited within the work with links when available

- The number of times the work has been cited on the database itself (with links) but also sometimes in other sources such as the WWW or in patents
- Citations alert service
- The ability to search using the references field
- Detailed metrics showing the breakdown of citation figures

In order to proceed with a citation search, one (or more) work should be selected to act as the starting point. It is preferable that this work is highly relevant to the subject matter so that any other works retrieved by the search are also likely to be relevant.

The nature of citation searching means that among the items of interest retrieved, there will inevitably be works that are not relevant or are of peripheral interest. It is therefore important that the information need is clearly defined together with the limits of the investigations (see Chapter 4) so that it can easily be decided whether or not an item is relevant.

Comprehensive citation searching including working forwards in time is difficult without a citation index.

When to stop

Citation searching can be a fascinating process, particularly when tracking developments in a chosen area. However, it is remarkably easy to find oneself following lines of investigation that are well beyond the scope of the original research. It can also be a time consuming process, and the researcher needs to be able to draw a halt to the proceedings, although, as more information is uncovered as the research progresses, a return to citation searching may be necessary. The signals for reaching the limits of a citation search are:

- The works that are being retrieved have already been discovered in the search
- The works being discovered are becoming less and less relevant

Electronic citation searching

Online citation searching is a powerful tool for the researcher. It allows easy searching of records that have been cited in the selected document as well as those which have later cited that document. The Web of Knowledge Citation Indexes have the facility for citation searches (using the Cited Reference Search option) using a combination of all or some of three fields:

- Cited author
- Cited work (that is, journal or book title, patent number, or another work)
- Cited year (the year the cited work was published; most effective when used in conjunction with the other search options)

For example, a search on WoK cited reference search using the author name Cartwright, M. and the year the cited work was published set as 1999 and 2000 results in seven hits, one of which has a link to a record stored on the WoK database. The article reference is:

> Cartwright, M. and Shepperd, M. (2000) An empirical investigation of an object-oriented software system, *IEEE Transactions on Software Engineering*, August, 26(8): 786–96.

Clicking on the link to this article then gives two figures in the full record:

- Cited references: 19
- Times cited: 21

'Cited references' indicates the number of references that Cartwright and Sheppard included in their article. 'Times cited' indicates the number of subsequent articles that have cited Cartwright and Sheppard's article. Of the 19 cited references, eight of them have records on WoK and therefore links to those records. All 21 of the 'times cited' records have links. The cited references date from 1988 to 1998 and the 'times cited' records from May 2002 to November 2006 (as at January 2007), demonstrating the backward and forward looking nature of citation searching. See Figure 7.2 for a diagrammatic representation of the timeline.

When checking out this same article on Scopus, the result shows that it has been cited 30 times in Scopus between 2001 and November 2006.

From this point, the cited references and 'times cited' information on any of the linked documents can be viewed. A chain of related records can then be retrieved, by continuing to view references in each subsequent document, but beware becoming lost and moving into irrelevant territory along the way.

Exactly what is retrieved using an online citation search depends on the database and the subscription. It may be possible to retrieve the full text (as on Science Direct), a citation with abstract or the basic citation of the document. If an item is linked using CrossRef or by their institution using other linking techniques, the searcher may be able to access the full text of the item (see Chapter 10).

Using an electronic citation search allows a search for any of the authors of a work, not only the first author.

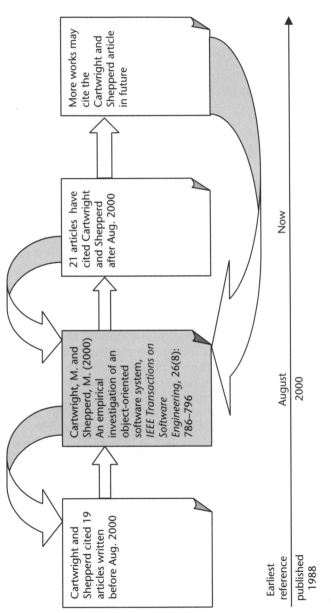

Figure 7.2 Timeline of citations

Patent citations

As well as a standard patent search, the UK Intellectual Property Office patent website[1] provides a link to the European Patent Office esp@cenet database which allows a search across over 20 European Patent Offices and the World Intellectual Property Service. Cited documents (i.e., those cited by the examiner in a search report), other equivalent versions of the document and groups of 'patent families' which are related to each other. From the results it is possible to view forward citations of the patent.

The US Patent Office Patent Full Text and Full Page Image Database[2] lists 'references cited' and also 'referenced by' information. The searcher is therefore able to retrieve records of subsequent patents that cite the selected patent and discover which patents the document has cited. The searcher may also search using the references field.

Problems associated with citation searching

Although citation searching using an electronic database is easier than following up references using printed resources, it is not without its problems:

- Consider the case of using the ISI Web of Knowledge citation indexes. Performing the search is straightforward; however, the resulting records will be those that are held on the WoK database. Although a large and multidisciplinary database, it does not include all records of everything ever published and so many relevant records will not be included in the results. Where possible, use more than one database.
- The inclusion of a citation in a document does not guarantee its quality. It should be evaluated like any other item (see Chapter 11).
- Bibliographic details of cited documents are given by authors and any errors are transferred into the database.
- Any bias in the coverage of the database will be reflected in the citations included.
- There may be a limit on the date of coverage of the database. For example, WoS Arts and Humanities Citation Index has backfiles from 1975 but the Science Citation Index Expanded extends back to 1900.
- A search using an author's name may retrieve many results, some of which might be irrelevant because they refer to another author with the same surname (and possibly initial). Use information such as the date, affiliation, and address to ascertain whether or not the author is the person intended.

One of the problems when performing a citation search is that of becoming lost in a long and convoluted trail of references. It is advisable to keep records of what has been discovered and where, so that the research trail does not become unmanageable or incomprehensible.

Cross-referencing

Be organized when tracking down references discovered via a work. This may require use of a mixture of print and electronic resources. For example, a record retrieved on Science Direct comprises the bibliographic citation, the full text (for subscribers), and a list of references cited in the article. The references may be a mixture of those which contain no links at all, those that link to an abstract only, and those that link to the full text of the article including references. Those that contain no links at all will have to be traced using library catalogues and other methods (see Chapters 8 and 10).

When working with print resources, it is advisable to copy any pages of references and mark copies with details of where they were published. This will aid any further chasing up later.

Bibliographies, lists of references, and footnotes should be used in order to cover the literature search comprehensively. It is this meticulous detective work that satisfies the researcher that they have been thorough.

British Standards

When searching for British Standards using the British Standards Online database,[3] the information given includes cross-references (with some hypertext links) to other standards. These references are all retrospective and do not include links to subsequent standards that have referred to the one currently being viewed. The standard itself may include a bibliography and a list of cross-references, but again, it is retrospective information. The database does, however, allow a search using the expanded search page to discover which standards have replaced the selected standard. For example, searching using the standard number 6634 (BS 6634:1985, ISO 6954–1984, published in August 1985) retrieves BS ISO 6954:2000 published 16 years later in May 2001.

CrossRef and OpenURLs

CrossRef is a collaborative development by a number of publishers which enables researchers to link directly from one article to another, regardless of publisher or publication. Libraries are increasingly using a system called OpenURLs which enables their users to link directly to their full text electronic resources when available from other databases. This is of immense benefit to the researcher who can easily follow up the references cited in an article.

Key points

- Citation searching is a means of investigating the influences on a work and the work it subsequently influenced
- A thorough search for information should include citation searching
- Keep to the defined scope of the research and do not become sidetracked
- Cross-references should be checked for completeness

Checklist

1 Check the references in the work(s) you are using and identify any you want to investigate further
2 Where might you check to see if the article(s) has/have been cited anywhere else? Can you find any actual citations of this/these article(s)?
3 Could any of the articles be defined as an original key work? If not, can you identify an original key work in the topic?
4 Using the references you discovered in step 2 above, are there any other works cited in those works which might be of interest?

8

Obtaining the full text

Introduction • Location of items at the home institution • Locating items not held in the home institution • Searching the catalogues of other collections • Locating electronic materials • Finding a commercial source of the material • Grey literature • Other sources for locating materials

Introduction

The title of this chapter includes the term 'full text'. Strictly, it should read 'full text or equivalent' as the resources may not comprise text, but images or other types. By this stage the researcher will have a list of relevant references to check out. Some of those references may have led immediately to the electronic full text (or equivalent) of the work by way of a link. This will have occurred if the full text was either (a) freely available or (b) part of an online collection to which the researcher is permitted access. It is likely, though, that some resources will be less easy to find. Some may prove very elusive.

Resource location is the process of identifying the whereabouts of the full content (text, image, recording, or other content) of the required information. There are many resources that allow the user to discover relevant items, such as abstract and indexing databases: often though, the user has to find the full content elsewhere. In these cases it is necessary to know the options available and the most appropriate tool utilized for the particular situation. The content may be hard copy or electronic (or both) and there are a number of possibilities for locating items. The choice of which to use will depend on:

- The format of the required content
- The permitted access to the resource (that is, selecting the most appropriate in the circumstances)

- Balancing the time factor and the distance the researcher is prepared to travel to obtain the item
- Whether the researcher is willing to spend money purchasing an item rather than borrowing it
- Whether the user's home library has the item or is willing to obtain it

This chapter is concerned with searching collections for specific items that the researcher has identified. Many of the sources mentioned may also prove useful for discovery of materials (see Chapter 5).

Most resource location (and discovery) can be achieved by scouring library catalogues and full text electronic databases. Other means may be necessary in certain circumstances where these tools are neither available nor appropriate. Archival catalogues often describe the collection rather than the individual items held within those collections. This chapter is concerned mainly with the use of online location tools. Figure 8.1 illustrates the locations of resources and common tools one would use to find the resource.

At this point in the search, the researcher should be in possession of full bibliographic or other descriptive details of the item(s) they require. Having this information will enable them to search the catalogues or other tools for full content access.

The RSLG report (RSLG 2003) includes the results of a survey which stated that '50 per cent of researchers think that their own university meets their research needs fairly well. 24 per cent think that their own university library meets their needs very well'. This is all well and good, but indicates that many researchers will be looking towards other sites for the supply of items they need. The Research Information Network is a strategic body set up to 'lead and co-ordinate new developments in the collaborative provision of research information for the benefit of researchers in the UK' (RIN 2007). The activities of this group should encourage better, more integrated research information provision and services in the future.

Resource location is not just about finding any provider that holds a copy of the required item: there is also the problem of finding the most *appropriate* copy. For example, the researcher may find that the British Library holds a copy of an item in its document supply catalogue. However, this is of no consequence if the user's own library provides immediate local access to it.

Many libraries and other centres allow access to their catalogues (or OPACs) to search their holdings and find the status of items (see Appendix 1). New systems are enabling users to search across other electronic resources at the same time as the catalogue.

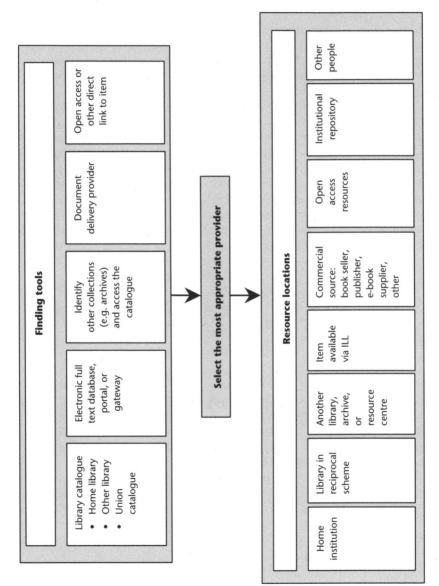

Figure 8.1 Resource locations and finding tools

Location of items at the home institution

The home library is probably where the researcher holds the fullest membership. If the researcher is a member of a university or other large institution, it is likely that first attempts at resource location will be made using their own library's OPAC and electronic resources. Those working at a distance to the home institution may wish to familiarize themselves with the catalogue of an information provider (such as a library or archive) at a more convenient location, but should be aware that there may be limits on the amount and types of materials that they can access (see Chapter 10).

The library catalogue is key to locating items, but there may be additional sources such as departmental collections or web pages, or special archives separate from the main collections. Some large institutions are multisite and have libraries or information centres at each or selected sites. Locating items may in this case be possible using a catalogue that covers all the libraries, or it may be necessary to use a number of different catalogues.

Locating items not held in the home institution

For high level research, it is unlikely that any one library will provide access to all the items required. Be prepared to look further afield for information sources. If the details of a particular item cannot be found at the home institution:

- Turn to an interlibrary loan or document supply service (see Chapter 10)
- Find an alternative location (either real or virtual) where the item is stored that will provide access to the item
- As a last resort abandon the search and find an alternative source of similar information which is in stock

It is this second option that will be dealt with here.

The options for resource location at an alternative location are:

- Searching the catalogues of other collections
- Locating another source of electronic materials
- Finding a commercial source of the material
- Using other people

These options will be dealt with in turn.

Searching the catalogues of other collections

Identifying collections

Before embarking on a search of another library, archive, or information store, it is necessary to identify appropriate **collections**. Such collections might be those of research libraries, specialist collections, national libraries, private collections, museums, archives, and so on. There will be some collections that will be obvious, for example, the national libraries and HE libraries. HERO provides information about and links to HE libraries (and other information sources) both in the UK and worldwide.

Other collections will be less well known. The *Aslib Directory of Information Sources in the United Kingdom* (Reynard 2004) is a comprehensive publication of many thousands of entries giving details of information collections and is a good starting point. Entries are alphabetical by organization and include those for institutes, commissions, associations, and government bodies. There is also a cross-referenced subject index.

Collection descriptions

Collection descriptions are a means of users finding collections that are of interest to them. They often include information such as the holdings and collection strengths. They can be used for resource discovery as well as resource location. Two example are the Archives Hub[1] (descriptions of archive collections) and the Backstage[2] performing arts gateway which allows the user to search for information about the locations of performing arts collections in the UK.

Research libraries

When locating items at research libraries, always have a clear idea of whether or not access to those sources will be allowed (see Chapter 10).

Searching OPACs and other catalogues

OPACs are generally easily accessible via the Web. Locating items at libraries which do not have an OPAC is more problematic.

Union or merged catalogues

Union or merged catalogues are invaluable as they allow searches of multiple catalogues simultaneously, therefore saving time. They can be a means of locating resources from a wide range of libraries. There are a number of initiatives in the UK by various consortia.

Serials Union Catalogue (SUNCAT)

The UK's freely available union catalogue of serials, SUNCAT (Serials UNion CATalogue),[3] provides a means of locating serials at a national level. It was first created in 2003 and development is continuing. SUNCAT claims to be 'the single most comprehensive source of information about serials holdings in the UK' (SUNCAT 2007).

Consortium of University Research Libraries (CURL) and COPAC

The members of CURL comprise over two dozen university and legal deposit libraries from around the UK and Ireland. One of the membership criteria for universities is those 'with a national or international reputation for scholarship and research information facilities' and those with 'extensive collections on a scale appropriate for the support of a broad range of research activity' (CURL 2003). The members of CURL acknowledge their standing as libraries with research collections that support the UK research community and they are committed to providing access to their holdings via their union catalogue and to their collections.

The CURL catalogue, COPAC,[4] is freely available on the Web. Users are able to search simultaneously across the catalogues of the member libraries to retrieve a full catalogue record, details the location(s) of holdings and, at some libraries, details of availability.

Other union catalogues

CAIRNS (Co-operative Academic Information Retrieval Network for Scotland)[5] is a union catalogue for 16 higher education and research institution libraries in Scotland (plus a handful of others) under the auspices of SCURL.

SALSER[6] is the union catalogue of serials held by members of SCURL. Users may search individual libraries, select groups by location, or search the entire content of the catalogue.

Inform25: the M25 consortium of HE libraries has created a virtual union catalogue of member institutions. The group comprises HE libraries in and around the London area. The InforM25 service enables simultaneous access to over 140 college and university library catalogues and a separate Union List of Serials (ULS)[7] of participating institutions.

Locating electronic materials

There are many initiatives aiming to simplify access to electronic documents and other e-resources. Locating electronic items is not always an easy task:

users should first check the holdings at their own institution and follow this by searching open access collections. Because it is a developing area, it is constantly changing. Library catalogues and other search systems may link directly to major open access collections, but this is not yet universal. There are many reputable journals which are freely available using the open access model: methods of easily finding such titles are improving.

e-Journals

It is common for large proportions of a large library's journal collection to be electronic. Titles are usually listed, and may be linked on the catalogue along with the print titles. Although a library may not stock or provide access to a given title, there are collections of open access journals being created and added to. These are journals for which there is no charge to the user and which can be accessed via the Web (see also open access below). Researchers can check the contents of such collections to find out whether they include the item they wish to locate. An important source of open access journals is the Directory of Open Access Journals (DAOJ)[8] (see below).

e-Books

e-Books is an area of rapid development. Most major publishers are producing (mainly reference) titles in electronic format. Libraries are increasingly purchasing electronic titles many of which are being added to their catalogues. However, not all libraries add individual titles to their catalogues. This means checking that library's e-book databases separately in order to find what is available. Locating a title can therefore be time consuming because of having to search a number of sources. Fortunately, records for individual titles of e-books are becoming easier for libraries to obtain and add to their catalogues and also e-book collections are being included in library metasearch systems which will search across multiple electronic resources provided by that library.

Open access

Access to scholarly information is an issue that is exercising many working at the cutting edge of research. Open access has two related facets: (1) open access journals which are free at the point of access, payment having been made earlier in the publishing process by for example, the author's institution or the funder of the research and (2) open access repositories where the research material is placed in an online store provided by, for example the researcher's institution, and made freely available via the Internet.

Increasing numbers of institutions and researchers are joining the drive towards open access and freely available **e-prints**. The sciences and social sciences are currently more represented than the arts and humanities. For example, RePEc[9] provides links to large amounts of free access research documents in the area of economics including working papers and journal articles, and UK PubMedCentral holds open access articles in biomedical and life sciences. This type of archive as a source for locating documents is valuable because of the ease of access to the material.

Institutions are developing open access online repositories to provide storage and access to their own research materials or output. The content may not be limited to e-prints and may also include conference and working papers, theses, and other forms of grey literature as well as images and datasets. It is possible to search across repositories which have registered with OAIster,[10] which harvests records from international open access repositories. An institutional repository search service for UK repositories is (at the time of writing) being developed by Intute in partnership with UKOLN and SHERPA.

Other freely available materials

Although subscriptions or pay per view are required for much information, there are some providers that allow free access to their sources. One example is UK National Statistics which provides free access to data and publications.

Finding a commercial source of the material

The researcher may be prepared to purchase an item personally or have other sources of funding for purchase. In these cases they would wish to find a commercial source of the item.

Booksellers

For books a local book shop or well known online bookseller may suffice, although rare or out of print materials may prove more problematic. In these cases the services of a specialist book store or an out of print supplier such as AbeBooks[11] or Bookfinder[12] may be needed. Locating such items can be difficult.

Journals and other resources

Journal articles and other document types may be available for pay per view delivery; for example, the British Library Direct service where articles can be searched for and then purchased online. In addition, the publisher's website or an online database can be used to locate items.

Other people

Personal contacts, such as a colleagues or supervisors, and discussion lists can be valuable means of locating information. Colleagues may not only know where items may be located, they may also be willing to lend personal copies of items (within copyright restrictions).

Grey literature

Locating grey literature can be a difficult and frustrating task. In the case of pamphlets, reports, and leaflets it is likely that no library will stock them and they may not have a bibliographic description. As institutional repositories develop, more grey literature may become easier to locate.

If an item is proving difficult to locate in a library, one solution can be to approach the company, individual, or department directly. For example, if the researcher has the details of a thesis from another country that is proving difficult to locate using conventional methods, running a search on the WWW can result in finding contact details for the academic department from where it originated or even personal contact details of the author. Of course, this method is somewhat unreliable as people move on and details change, but it is possible that an individual might be willing to send copies of publications to the researcher.

Other sources for locating materials

EU information

Although much European Union information is freely available on the EU websites the researcher looking for other EU materials may find what they require at one of the 44 European Documentation Centres (EDCs) in the UK or one of the European Public Information Centres (EPICs). Details can be found on the European Information Network in the UK[13] website.

Newspapers

One of the problems for libraries of storing back copies of newspapers is the space that they take up and their physical shape, making storage and shelving (and consequently retrieval) difficult. To address these difficulties many libraries retain copies of newspapers in a microform format or via an electronic provider. The British Library's Newspaper Collection is the UK's major provider of back copies of newspapers, including national and provincial titles. There is a dedicated catalogue for this collection.

Official publications

The BOPCRIS database includes a collections directory to help users find the location of their chosen documents. The National Archives catalogue allows users to search for documents and find the location of many in the UK.

Historical records, archives, and manuscripts

The UK National Register of Archives[14] provides information about manuscripts and historical records relating to British history and their locations.

The ARCHON directory gives contact and location details of the archives which 'substantial collections of manuscripts' (National Archives 2007) included in the NRA, including those that are not located in the UK.

The Archives Hub[15] is a national gateway of descriptions of archive and manuscript collections held in UK HE and colleges. The site provides information about the collections with links directly to many sites for further information and catalogues.

Access to Archives (A2A)[16] gives access to many collection descriptions of local archives held in England and Wales.

SCONE (Scottish Collections Network Extension)[17] provides descriptions of collections held in Scottish libraries, museums, and archives, and collections about Scottish topics held elsewhere.

AIM25[18] is being created to provide online access to collection level descriptions of the archives of over 50 higher education institutions and learned societies within the Greater London area. It is under development and funded by the Research Support Libraries Programme (RSLP). Participating institutions include the University of London, other universities located within the M25 consortium of academic libraries and some of the royal colleges and societies of medicine and science in London.

Key points

- Resource location is about finding the most appropriate source of information
- Search catalogues including union catalogues
- Open access materials might be linked to library catalogues, but may need searching separately
- The location of items, especially grey literature, may involve using printed catalogues and contacting people personally as well as online searching

---

Checklist

1   Have you checked all possible catalogues and online sources at your home institution including online full text e-journal and e-book collections?
2   Are any of the materials you require available open access either in an open access journal or via an open access repository?
3   Are you aware of any relevant specialist collections or archives?

9

Using the World Wide Web for research

Introduction • Means of locating information on the WWW • Accessing the selected site • Subject gateways • Using search engines • Evaluating information found on the WWW • Some useful tips

Introduction

The World Wide Web (WWW or Web) forms only one part of the Internet. The Internet is a multiplex of networks comprising elements such as:

- email
- discussion groups and newsgroups
- the WWW
- a means of file transfer

This chapter deals with the WWW part of the Internet, the freely available resources it contains, and locating and evaluating those resources. The WWW provides access to text documents, graphics, moving images, and hyperlinks leading to further information.

Unlike some other publishing processes, items on the WWW may be published without review or any other editorial procedure. This means that the quality and reliability of the material can be questionable. It is the user's responsibility to ensure that any information used is of a suitable quality. To this end, it is advisable to become proficient in Web evaluation techniques and not an indiscriminate Web user.

The WWW is undoubtedly a valuable research tool. There is a large amount of high quality information freely available: there is also much dubious material. The skill lies in distinguishing between the two.

It is likely that an answer to a query can be found on the Web. It may also be true that information can be found much quicker simply by picking up a printed source close to hand. The choice of source can be dependent on a number of factors:

- Location proximity: where does the user physically have to be to access the information?
- Time: the time taken either to log on to a computer or obtain the hard copy to access the information
- Currency: although Web sources can be kept up to date easily, this does not always happen in practice

The most appropriate choice is that which is most convenient and relevant to the current query and situation.

Intute Internet tutorials

Intute provides valuable training and guides on the use of the Internet including two Internet tutorials:

1 A Virtual Training Suite for Internet research skills in selected subject areas. Each subject includes sections on subject specific websites, a tutorial in how to search the Web effectively and also on how to evaluate websites.
2 The Internet Detective, a part of the Virtual Training Suite, which 'offers practical advice on evaluating the quality of websites and highlights the need for care when selecting online information sources to inform university or college work' (Place et al. 2006). This tutorial includes help on topics such as scholarly resources, copyright, and plagiarism and evaluating information found on the Web.

See also subject gateways below.

Means of locating information on the WWW

The information required may be located on the Web using one or more of a selection of different location tools. The options are:

- typing the URL in the address box
- using a gateway or portal
- using a search engine

The choice of which tool to use will depend on whether the researcher would like to access:

1 A specific website where the URL is known
2 A specific website where the URL is unknown
3 A website on a chosen topic that has been selected by a specialist
4 A selection of websites on a chosen topic
5 A relevant website from no particular provider or source

Where a URL is known, the researcher can easily type in the address to access the site. For options 2 and 5, a search engine would be a suitable solution. Options 3, 4, and 5 could make the use of a gateway or directory.

One can make an educated guess at the URL of certain websites if the precise address is unknown. Commonly used formats of URL contain elements such as:

- .com or .co.uk for a commercial company
- .ac.uk or .edu for higher education sites (respectively in the UK and the US)
- .gov.uk for UK government sites
- .org for other organizations such as professional bodies or charities

An abbreviation at the end of the URL can indicate a country for example .fr for France or .de for Germany.

Accessing the selected site

Once the selected or a relevant site has been found, access to it may or may not be straightforward. Sites will fall into one or more of the following categories:

- Freely available – the resource is free of charge, with no restrictions on access
- Conditionally free – all or part of the resource is freely available under set conditions. The conditions might relate to the institution or require registration
- Institutional subscription – access to the resource is for members (or other entitled individuals) of an institution which holds a subscription or licence for the resource. This may mean that access is only available from computers at a specified location such as those at certain institutions such as a university or company
- Commercially available such as pay per view

Conditions of access may limit usage to a specified number of concurrent users. Some sites provide limited access, perhaps by way of a guest user's option which allows access to some, but not all, of the resource.

Subject gateways

Internet gateways are subject-based collections of online information sources located at external sites. They often take the form of a directory and have usually been selected and evaluated by a subject specialist or information professional.

The examples of gateways given here have been created with academic users as their target audience although freely available to anyone.

Intute is a gateway which allows the user to search across the whole site or within four broad subject areas. It has useful functions such as marking and email records facilities.

> Intute is a free online service providing you with access to the very best Web resources for education and research. The service is created by a network of UK universities and partners. Subject specialists select and evaluate the websites in our database and write high quality descriptions of the resources.
>
> (Intute 2006)

Wikipedia,[1] the online encyclopedia, has become a favourite source of information for many. While it does contain much valuable and interesting information, users should bear in mind that the content is not always necessarily edited and verified by experts.

Portals

A portal is a refined gateway which can be personalized and customized according to the user's status and preferences. They may include features such as the ability to cross-search multiple databases, the use of personalized alerting services, and the ability to select the resources included. They often include means for resource discovery, email access, and online discussion. Some probe deeper than others (sometimes known as thick portals) and may, for example, allow users to link directly to the full text of a journal article provided by an external supplier rather than merely linking to the main search page (Dolphin et al. 2002). A gateway is static in that it appears the same to all users.

The JISC describes a portal as a 'possibly personalised, common point of access where searching can be carried out across one or more than one resource and the amalgamated results viewed' (JISC 2007a). An institution may set up a portal for its members as a means of presenting appropriate information and services to defined groups of its staff and students. Portals are being used together with other services such as VREs within institutions so that users are able to find and use resources and services easily and seamlessly without having to move from one source to another.

Using search engines

What is a search engine?

The WWW is a conglomeration of diverse information with no imposed order, indexing, or system of storage. This means that, unlike a well ordered library where all items are catalogued, classified, and shelved in a logical order, finding relevant documents on the WWW can feel like searching for a needle in a vast and rapidly growing haystack.

A search engine is a device for locating Internet sites based on criteria input by the user. They are usually freely available, although some require a subscription (for example, Northern Light Enterprise search engine[2]). Although each engine would have the user believe that it is the best and covers most, if not all, of the Web, the reality is somewhat different. Most Web searchers have a favourite engine and it is difficult to break the habit of using that engine without considering any others.

The search engines considered here are those designed to search the general WWW rather than those that search within a particular website.

Numbers of search engines

Searchers can generally name a handful of well known search engines. In fact, there are many hundreds freely available. They differ in their methods of searching, the extent of the Web they cover, how they display the results and other features. It is worth comparing engines and the searcher should be prepared to use a selection if they do not retrieve the results they require.

Features of search engines

Methods of locating information

The two main types of search method are (1) allowing the user to type in a query and (2) directories which allow the user to drill down through categories to reach the desired site. The directory option is constructed by human beings who determine the most appropriate category for each site.

1 Engines that allow the user to type in a query. Within this category there are variants:

- free text search
- assisted search
- natural language search

    Free text searching allows the user to input the query using a command box or similar. The user can be highly specific and incorporate Boolean search terms and other operators. For the expert searcher, this can be the most reliable and satisfying means of searching. Examples of engines that include this option are Alta Vista[3] and All the Web.[4]

An assisted search might be provided which has boxes for the user to complete. These might be to find:

- all the words
- any of the words
- the exact phrase

and are in fact using Boolean logic (see Chapter 6).

Natural language searching allows the user to input the query as if they were asking a verbal question. For example the search query might be, 'Why did Henry the Eighth execute Anne Boleyn?' or 'How can I access the Library of Congress catalogue?'

2 Directories. Directory or index search engines work using a hierarchical system of subjects. The subject can be focused until the exact topic is found. For example, Yahoo Search Directory[5] lists around 14 topics including government, health, regional, and science. Clicking on the government link leads to a page containing 'top categories':

- countries
- law
- military
- politics
- US government

It is possible to select additional categories such as 'embassies and consulates' and 'international organizations'.

Directories are useful when the searcher wants a selection of sites about a particular topic, but for sites that include specific text anywhere on the page, a free text engine is preferable. Some engines are hybrids and offer both options.

Meta search engines

Meta or multisearch engines (sometimes called meta crawlers) provide the means of searching across a number of engines in one operation. It is a useful method of spreading the search over a wider area of the Web. For example, the Ixquick[6] search engine can search up to 12 engines (including Alta Vista/ AllTheWeb, Ask/Teoma, WiseNut, and Gigablast). A search results in a list of retrieved hits, each showing on which engine it was found, and the ranking of the site on that engine. Kartoo[7] searches around 14 engines and selects some for the search, although the user can opt for a search covering all the engines.

A drawback of such engines is that truncation and wildcard characters are unlikely to be identical on all the engines used for the search.

Targeted engines

Some engines are designed to be country specific such as Lycos Français[8] or the Finnish engine WWW.Fi[9]. Others are targeted at specific topics such as medicine or finance.

Google Scholar and Windows Live Academic Search

In a book such as this, mention must be made of Google Scholar,[10] Google's attempt to provide a search engine focused on academic literature including articles, theses, and books. It must be stressed that at the time of writing it is still described as a 'beta' version and, although useful, is not comprehensive. There are a number of features of Google Scholar which are of great interest to researchers such as links to cited items, a related articles feature, and links to library catalogues. Publishers can arrange for their publications to be indexed by Google Scholar and libraries can arrange for direct full text links to the electronic resources they provide for their users. Another feature allows searchers to find the whereabouts of a copy of the item.

The Microsoft search engine for scholarly items is Windows Live Academic Search.[11] This service is building in features such as 'author live links' which allow users to find other items included in the system by the same author. Another useful feature is that of the split screen: search results on the left and a preview of the selected result on the right. The content included in Windows Live Academic Search is fed to it directly from the publishers. Like Google Scholar, inclusion does not mean that searchers will have access to the full text – unless items are freely available, access remains available only to those with permission (such as subscribers). This service is currently flagged as a 'beta' version.

These are services to monitor to see how they develop and if they become widely accepted and well used tools by the scholarly community.

Quick and advanced search options

Many of the larger search engines have both quick and advanced (or 'more precision') search options. The quick search is useful when using a small number of search terms or phrase(s) and when the researcher is not too concerned about the numbers or relevance of the results. If the search term is an unusual word or a phrase, the quick search can be an easy method of obtaining relevant results. It may be possible to use Boolean operators, wildcards, or phrase marks in the quick search box for increased precision.

The advanced search option allows for more precision in the results and increased relevance. It may allow features such as selecting the language of the results or searching for selected domains or types of document such as PDF. For example, a phrase search performed using the Google UK[12] search engine (using the 'Pages from the UK' option) resulted in the following. Quick search:

- Query: "internal combustion engine"
- Numbers of results: 116,000

Advanced search:

- Query: "internal combustion engine"
- Language limit: English
- Format limit: Adobe Acrobat PDF
- Date limit: pages updated in the past three months
- Occurrences: return pages where the terms appear in the title
- Usage rights: not filtered by licence
- Numbers of results: 226

Default settings

When typing in two or more search terms the searcher should be aware of the default setting of the engine, whether it is a Boolean AND or OR. The results will differ depending on the setting. This information is usually given in the 'Help' function of the engine. Always check the 'Help' function to be assured that the results are what were expected and to take advantage of the engine's features.

Interface

The interfaces of search engines vary: some have text and graphics in every available inch of space, while others are cleaner looking. Some have moving images, such as advertisers' promotional material, while others include no obvious commercial material. Home pages vary from those that easily fit into a window to those that require much scrolling to view the entire page. It may be possible to customize the view if there is a My Search Engine option such as that on Yahoo. Customizing allows the searcher to select the areas that are displayed, retaining only the parts that are of interest, and may include an alerting facility. Preferences are a matter for the individual.

The advanced search option may not be obvious if the link is in tiny text.

An engine such as Kartoo has an interesting method of displaying results by providing a pictorial representation (although a typical list format is also available). This is a diagram of how the selected sites link to each other by topic. The results interface also provides a list of topics, allowing the searcher to narrow down their search by defining relevant topics. Kartoo also provides a basic search history facility for each query.

As search engines become more sophisticated, more features are being added such as suggestions for additional searches, suggested keywords as you type, and for related sources such as images and blogs.

Comparing the results

The results pages of search engines vary as much as the home pages. Results are displayed in different orders, with varying amounts of information for evaluation of the results and with differing 'busyness' of display.

Relevance and ranking of results

Probably the criterion that is of paramount importance to the researcher is that of the relevance of the results retrieved. The ranking can be important if there are many hits as it is unlikely that the searcher will trawl through all the results.

Engine designers are constantly attempting to improve search mechanisms so that the results displayed have high relevance. This does, of course, depend on the search query input by the searcher. There are factors such as where on the page the terms appear (a result is likely to be more relevant if the term is in the title), the metadata (hidden data that describes the page), the number of links to a page and the engine's ability to counter any scurrilous tricks attempted by web page publishers to make their page rank highest. Sponsored links appear at the top of many results pages.

Ranking depends on the search engines' perception of how relevant a page is. Again, the engines differ in how they achieve this.

The results page

The results page displays short extracts designed to enable assessment of whether or not a site is relevant and needs further investigation. They vary in the amount of information they provide and some have additional features such as 'related search' links or provide the date when the site was last refreshed and a list of terms for refining the search. Such features can make the search easier and more relevant, for example, Google provides a 'search within results' option to help narrow down the search. Ask.com[13] offers a number of options to narrow the search. Clusty,[14] sorts the results into groups or 'clusters' of related resources.

Reliability of search engines

Many search engines will retrieve hits quickly and with a high degree of relevance. However, there are some issues of which the searcher should be aware. For example, some engines construct their databases using a spider or Web crawler. The crawler wanders around the WWW gathering sites as it goes. This may take some time, which means that a lot can change between one visit from the spider and the next and the average age of the pages displayed by search engines varies.

Not all engines will retrieve certain types of files such as PDF documents. See the invisible Web below.

The directories of directory search engines are compiled by humans. This means that the user's opinion of where a site may be listed may not match that of the directory compiler.

The invisible Web

The vast numbers of pages indexed by search engines or added to directories can engender a false sense of security for the searcher. In fact, there are large parts of the WWW which are not easily accessed by engines and which have been called 'the invisible Web'. Sites that may be included in this category could be:

- Individual databases containing digital resources or records
- Password protected pages
- Documents in PDF or formats other than html
- URLs with no other links leading to them
- Content which is not text based (such as images)
- Dynamic content

There are attempts to rectify the inaccessibility of some invisible sites such as including PDF documents in the searches. This was major step forward for researchers as many scholarly publications are produced in this format.

Selecting an engine

There is such a choice of engines on offer with many variables between engines, that it is understandable why many searchers remain faithful to one particular favourite. Some searches will benefit from being run on a subject or country specific engine. For example, Scirus[15] is a science-specific search engine (from the publishers, Elsevier) and the International Directory of Search Engines[16] lists a collection of country specific engines. Although the engine selected remains the preference of the researcher, some criteria for choosing a type of search engine are those given in Table 9.1.

Table 9.1 Some criteria for selecting search engines

Task	Type of engine
Searcher has prepared key terms	Free text
Searcher knows of a specific site they wish to access	Free text
Searcher wishes to seek terms within the text	Free text
Searcher wishes to use a number of key terms including synonyms	Free text
Searcher wishes to input multiple terms but is unsure of connectors	Assisted free text
Searcher wishes to input the query as a question	Natural language
Searcher wishes to browse a topic	Directory/Index (or Gateway)
Searcher wishes to obtain an overview of sites in a subject area	Directory/Index (or Gateway)
Searcher wishes to perform as wide a search as possible	Meta engine
Searcher is concerned with sites from a specific country	Country specific (or Gateway)
Searcher is concerned with sites in a particular subject area	Subject specific (or Gateway)
Sites may form part of the invisible Web	PDF compliant, invisible Web engine (or Gateway)

If one search engine does not produce suitable results, it is worth re-running the search on another.

Finding out more about search engines

There are sites designed to help the user find out more about using search engines and provide interesting comparison statistics (although not always obtained using rigorous scientific methods). Pages vary in how up to date they are.

- Phil Bradley's Web pages (Bradley 2008)
- SearchEngineWatch (Lieb 2007)
- Search Engine Showdown (Notess 2007)

Evaluating information found on the WWW

Because documents retrieved on the WWW are such a mixture of quality ranging from the scholarly and reliable to the untrustworthy, researchers should equip themselves with strategies for evaluating the content they discover. Some sites are obviously designed for commercial purposes or are overtly light-hearted. Others can be more difficult to ascertain whether they are reliable scholarly information sources or whether there is a hidden agenda or include unreliable claims.

Work through the criteria for each site under consideration. If unsure about the quality of a site, ignore it or make it quite clear that the information is unsupported or questionable.

Criteria for evaluating websites

Websites may be evaluated using the following criteria:

- Ownership: sites which do not make this information clear should not be trusted. The author could be anybody. Although corporate owners can be biased, their intentions are usually clear.
- Authority: if the user cannot trust the author or the corporate body who published the site, then they should not use the information.
- Currency: a site that is no longer being updated, including the hyperlinks, should not be trusted. The information may be incorrect.
- Quality of content: judging quality can be difficult, especially on pages that appear plausible. On closer inspection the searcher may find there are no supporting data for opinions or facts. Content can be biased in a number of ways (as in any publication), for example, political, academic (that is, supporting only one school of thought), commercial, and so on.
- Intended audience: information should be at the right level.

The criteria can be judged by the searcher considering the following questions.

Ownership:

1 Is it clear who is the author of the site/page?
2 Is there a corporate owner of the information?
3 Are there contact details for the page owner?

Authority:

1 What authority does the author possess?
2 Was the searcher made aware of the site from a reliable source?

Currency:

1 How up to date is the information?
2 Are the Web links on the page working?

Quality of content:

1 Are claims supported by reliable evidence?
2 What is the quality of the use of language and grammar?
3 Do Web links lead to high quality and reliable sites?
4 Is the information biased in any way?

Intended audience:

1 Who is the intended audience?
2 Is the site a vehicle for commercial promotional material?
3 Does the site include advertising?
4 Are you being asked for money?
5 See also Chapter 11

The main point is to be critical.

Some useful tips

Expert use of the WWW takes practice and also a willingness to become aware of the issues and options available. The following list contains some helpful hints that make using the WWW more efficient:

- To find the terms searched for on a Web page use the computer's find function. This may be in the Edit menu or there might be a hot key/shortcut such as using Control Key + F. This function can save scrolling down a long page.
- Many major engines provide a 'search within' function to narrow down a search without re-running it. This enables searching of the retrieved results.
- Bookmarking a site (or adding a site to a list of favourites) is a useful option when the searcher wishes to return to the site at a later time. When returning to a site using this method, refresh or reload the page to ensure that the latest version is displayed.

Key points

- Gateways are a means of quickly finding relevant and usually trustworthy information
- Search engines vary in their features, presentation and relevance ranking
- Be prepared to use more than a single search engine
- Information found on the WWW should be evaluated for reliability

---

Checklist

1   Have you considered using more than one search engine?
2   Have you recorded detailed references of where you found the information?
3   Have you been critical enough of what you have retrieved on the WWW?

10

Accessing materials

*Introduction • Accessing physical materials held at the home institution
• e-Resources available via the home institution • Using other libraries
• Document delivery services • Open access to scholarly publications
• Persistent identifiers • Accessing other sources of information*

Introduction

By this stage of the information seeking process the researcher will have the
full details of the item (whether physical or electronic) and its location (if not
being obtained using an interlibrary loan service).

There are many issues related to the access of items such as:

- Borrowing rights
- Subscriptions and authentication for use of electronic resources
- Viewing, saving, and printing electronic items
- Restrictions on use of materials obtained from other libraries
- Initiatives such as open access
- Entitlement and cost of interlibrary loans/document supply
- Potential difficulties in accessing grey literature
- Agreements between publishers regarding direct access from a database to
  full text
- Sensitive information
- Time delays

Accessing physical materials held at the home institution

The researcher's primary source is likely to be the home institution. For those working at a distance, another source may prove more convenient, but the home site is the one that will provide access to subscription electronic resources (at least, those subscribed to by the institution) and may offer the most comprehensive borrowing rights. There may be a special arrangements for distance learners to enable them to obtain resources from the home or other libraries.

The researcher will have borrowing and access rights agreed by their institution and, for the most part, will be able to access materials at no personal cost. They should become proficient in using their own library's catalogue so that they can be sure whether or not an item is in stock and not waste time attempting to access it elsewhere.

Some libraries are multisite and the user might have to make special arrangements to obtain items from sister sites. For example, there may be a regular delivery service of items requested from other sites such as remote stores.

Closed access libraries require that the user request the item(s) and then wait for them to be fetched by a member of library staff. There is a time factor involved here which should be taken into account when planning the research and requesting such items.

Even at the home institution there may be items that are designated restricted access or held in a closed access store. Special arrangements for access then have to be made.

e-Resources available via the home institution

Links from databases to full text

Depending on publishers and licensing agreements, users can increasingly access the full text of an item directly from a bibliographic database. Some databases such as Science Direct or Ebsco Online are stores of full text articles which the searcher is able to discover by running a search on the database. They can then access the full text if they either have appropriate authentication or are willing to pay using a credit card for direct document delivery.

Links to full text rely on the subscriber's entitlements. As the electronic environment grows, more agreements and options are being put into place as publishers and database providers negotiate deals and libraries provide links using their own catalogues. ISI WoK, for example, offers two additional services for HE:

- *Holdings*: links from WoK to the library's own (and other catalogues such as COPAC). If the catalogue includes any linked URLs of electronic titles subscribed to by the library the user may access these titles even if they are not the subject of an agreement between ISI and the publisher.
- *ISI links:* links directly from WoK full records to the online full text (where it exists) of participating publishers. The links are controlled by the institution and reflect the institution's entitlements.

Issues related to electronic provision of materials

It is usual to be able to save, print, email, and/or fax items. Users may not be able to copy text in a document that is in PDF. There may be a choice of full text format such as HTML (Hypertext Markup Language) or PDF.

One of the difficulties with electronic resources is the different methods of proceeding from discovery of the resource to obtaining the item in full. The simplest method is to find the required resource, click on a link, and have the full item presented with no interim stages. However, having found the details of the required item it may then be necessary to transfer to a separate resource from another provider with a different interface to access the full text.

As stated earlier, the transition from resource discovery, via resource location to the full text is becoming increasingly seamless, with access possible from one resource to another without any interim steps.

e-Books

Many institutions offer some book titles electronically. At present, there are a number of different methods of achieving this and decisions have to be taken regarding which suppliers to use (they vary in their methods of provision), which access mechanism to adopt (via PC – personal computer – or handheld device) and how details should be incorporated on the library catalogue. Some libraries include all individual titles of collections in their catalogues, others require the researcher to search the e-book collections separately or use the library's federated search tool.

A number of major e-book collections have been purchased or licensed by the JISC to make them affordable to UK HE and FE institutions. These tend to be (at time of writing) either reference or historical collections. One example is EEBO (Early English Books Online) which covers a multitude of disciplines and comprises over 125,000 titles from 1473 to 1700. Researchers should regularly check their library's e-book provision as there might be titles valuable to their research found within the collections. The collections may change regularly as titles are added and new collections are made available.

There are some e-book titles that are available freely such as those listed on Project Gutenberg[1] (although readers should check the copyright even here as advised on the website). Titles tend to be older publications.

Using other libraries

As the UK moves towards a coordinated approach for research support, there are more arrangements for reciprocal access and borrowing between university libraries. If the home library does not stock the item required, it might be obtained at an institution where there is a reciprocal access and/or borrowing agreement. This may be a local, regional, or national arrangement. A researcher wishing to take advantage of this type of arrangement must first search the appropriate library or union catalogue to check holdings.

The SCONUL (Society of College, National and University Libraries) Research Extra[2] scheme allows research students and academic staff to access and borrow items from other participating libraries (currently most UK HE institutions). Users should be aware that electronic resources are not included in the scheme. SCONUL also promotes other access and borrowing schemes.

National libraries like the British Library permit researchers access to their resources: users should check details such as conditions of use and ordering procedures and times. There may be access restrictions on rare materials with special conservation requirements.

Examples of reciprocal schemes between institutions and other regional, local, or associated institutions include the RIDING schemes arranged by a consortium of universities in Yorkshire and Humberside, NoWAL libraries in the northwest of England and that arranged in Scotland between the libraries of Glasgow, Strathclyde, Glasgow Caledonian, and Paisley Universities.

When considering using any reciprocal scheme, the researcher should first check the libraries that are currently participating in a scheme and any restrictions on access and borrowing imposed by those libraries. Some collections may be valuable or rare and access might only be allowed to those who are deemed eligible.

Document delivery services

For ILL many libraries use the British Library's Document Supply Centre (BLDSC), run from Boston Spa in Yorkshire. This offers a number of different services to which registered users have access. It is a separate service to that of the British Library at St Pancras in London.

A journal article requested via interlibrary loan is usually provided as a photocopy that the user may keep. If the researcher has requested more than one article from a single issue of a journal, then the whole issue will be loaned in order to comply with copyright law. Copies of book chapters can sometimes be supplied (dependent on copyright) otherwise the entire volume is supplied. Allowable usage of items may vary depending on restrictions set by the owner of the item. For example, an item may be restricted to library use only: the borrower may not be able to take the item out of the library which arranged the interlibrary loan. Books can be borrowed for a set period and renewal might not be extended. Heavy penalties are incurred if ILL items are not returned by the given date.

When requesting an item via interlibrary loan and signing the copyright declaration the user is agreeing to use the item in compliance with the terms of the copyright agreement, for example, use only for personal research or not having been previously supplied with the same item. A library can acquire items via interlibrary loan for multiple users, but a higher, copyright cleared, fee is charged.

The most common formats of interlibrary loan are books or articles, but the user may find that they are sent a microform, particularly if a thesis has been requested (although this is set to change). The usage instructions on these items should be read carefully as there may be guidelines regarding printing and other instructions. There are sometimes options for online delivery and electronic access.

Although a photocopy of a journal article obtained from the British Library may be delivered within a few days, some take longer to arrive. Sometimes the British Library does not possess the item that has been requested. In such a case, there may be a delay while it obtains the item. Delays may also occur if an item is in heavy demand and a waiting list has developed or it is being obtained from abroad. In any case, requesting an item via interlibrary loan will result in having to wait to obtain the item and the research should be planned around this.

Document supply services can be used to locate and access documents. The British Library[3] catalogue has a separate search option (within catalogue subset search) for items it is able to supply remotely. Services such as Ingenta (the online or fax/ariel articles options) and DocDel[4] provide online document delivery, but charge for this service and the British Library provides a payment document delivery service, British Library Direct. A directory of document suppliers is maintained by DocDel.net (although it is worth checking open access archives where documents may be freely available). A separate index lists suppliers in main subject areas and a list of UK suppliers: many provide a search facility of their database of documents. If an item is located on an e-journal database, yet the institution does not subscribe to that title, it might still be obtainable by paying personally for document delivery (if provided) by credit card. Journal publishers sometimes offer a pay per view document delivery service such as that provided by the scientific publisher, Kluwer[5] or Elsevier STM publishers via their Science Direct[6] service or by a supplier such as Ebsco.

Open access to scholarly publications

In learned institutions around the UK and globally, researchers are creating records of their work including articles, data sets, first drafts of papers, and so on. There is a wealth of information locked away which, if made available to other researchers, could substantially change the culture and speed of research developments. The opening up of access to scholarly publications is being developed globally.

e-Prints: electronic copies of scholarly papers

The e-print revolution started in 1991 with a computer system for storing and providing access to scholarly papers. This repository (now at Cornell University) is known as arXiv[7] and the content is in the disciplines of physics, mathematics, non-linear science and computer science. Papers can be submitted when the author chooses (which can be immediately upon completion) and once in the archive, are open access, that is, freely available to users.

An e-print can be described as a scholarly publication, often a journal article, in electronic form. The content could be a research or conference paper, the results of experiments or other research. They are either pre-prints (that is prior to being refereed) or post-prints (peer reviewed items). These electronic papers may be stored in an e-print repository or archive, and their electronic nature allows for more rapid dissemination than the traditional route of publishing.

The JISC in the UK has invested in many projects and other work to support and develop repositories and the underlying infrastructure, services, and advice for providers. These include projects concerned with 'fostering the creation of institutional e-print repositories within the UK' and 'the development of new types of services that provide some kind of unified access to the content of such repositories' (Day 2003). e-Print repositories are becoming increasingly common as part of an institution's archive of research information (Day 2003).

Documents relating to research prior to publication are of great value to researchers. Although some would not wish their work to be available either in an early draft or before being reviewed (particularly in the medical sciences), there are many who value the opportunity for others to access such publications. Academic documents such as these are usually available at no cost to the user: the visibility and impact of the work is one of the greatest benefits for the author.

The results of this literature being freed up is that researchers will have immediate access to a larger corpus of research literature. As Theo Andrew stated,

> individual scholars, seeing an opportunity to distribute their work easily
> to a potentially wide audience and, as a by-product, raise their research

profiles, have also seized the opportunity to use new technology by posting research material online.

(Andrew 2003)

Institutional repositories

Since the development and availability of free e-print software, universities are developing internal repositories for self-archived (that is, deposited by the author or their representative) items of research output. This action can free up publications, certainly within the institution, but, by complying with OAI (Open Archives Initiative) protocol and allowing external access, can release findings to the global research community, thereby raising the impact of the publication. These repositories may contain diverse items including e-prints, data, conference papers, working drafts, and other grey literature as well as moving images and other resources.

Institutional repositories may or may not be open access: some sections may limited to small groups. Most large UK universities have set up an institutional repository.

Other repositories

Some repositories are those dedicated to a single discipline such as the arXiv physics repository or RePEc (Research Papers in Economics).[8] A major e-print resource for scientists and engineers based in the US is the E-print Network[9] which provides the means of searching for e-prints in these disciplines.

Most repositories are searchable using major search engines. Other useful sources include OpenDOAR (Directory of Open Access Repositories),[10] ROAR (Registry of Open Access Repositories),[11] and OAIster.[12]

The Open Archives Initiative

The OAI (Open Archives Initiative)[13] is promoted by those committed to the increased dissemination of scholarly materials including information users, providers, and brokers/mediators. It focuses on the technological framework and protocols required to make this possible, rather than the content or economic issues of scholarly communication. The OAI promotes sharing of content, compliance with the OAI protocol, and the development of an international network of institutional repositories.

OAI compliant e-print repositories ease access to their content which can be used by anyone (Simpson 2002). Repositories that comply with the OAI protocol now amount to over 100, dispersed around the world. Major centres include:

- arXiv (see above)
- BioMed Central[14]

- Directory of Open Access Journals (DOAJ)[15]
- Public Library of Science (PLoS)[16]
- PubMed,[17] PubMed Central,[18] and UK PMC[19]

BioMed Central

BioMed Central is a provider of free access, peer reviewed biomedical research literature. This UK-based publisher encourages the creation of new open access journals and offers publication services to research groups.

The Directory of Open Access Journals (DOAJ)

The DOAJ was created by Lund University Libraries. It contains information about the journals which are listed on its database, and links to the full text of many of the journals from the DOAJ site. There are hundreds of journals included and the content is growing. The subject coverage is in the fields of science, human sciences, and humanities and papers are either peer reviewed or editorially controlled to retain quality. The DOAJ's definition of an open access journal is one that uses 'a funding model that does not charge readers or their institutions for access' (DOAJ 2007).

The Public Library of Science (PLoS)

PLoS is a not for profit organization that is working towards making scientific and medical literature open access. Its goals include providing 'unlimited access to the latest scientific research' and to 'facilitate research, informed medical practice, and education by making it possible to freely search the full text of every published article' (PLoS 2007). Users may use the material for any lawful purpose including downloading, distributing, and linking to the full text. The authors have the right to retain control over the integrity of their work and the right to be correctly acknowledged and cited.

PLoS is publishing journals (PLoS Biology first issued October 2003 and PLoS Medicine mid-2004) to which users have free access. There are plans to publish further titles, all of which will be peer reviewed and freely available. Authors (or their institutions) are, however, required to pay to offset publishing costs.

PubMed and PubMed Central, UKPMC

PubMed contains citations of articles in the field of biomedical science including links to many in full text. PubMed Central (PMC) is a full text archive of journals in the life sciences from the US National Library of Medicine. PMC is running a digitization programme to add non-electronic back issues to the archive. UK PMC (UK PubMed Central) is a UK mirror of PMC and also provides a means of submitting manuscripts for deposit in the archive using the UKMSS (UK manuscript submission system).

Persistent identifiers

Electronic publications have the advantage that any citations can link directly to the (electronic) full text of the work referenced. However, the inclusion of links may cause difficulties for both author and reader. One problem lies in the ephemeral and transient nature of the Internet. URLs change, links become broken or redundant and the reader is no longer able to find or access the documents to which the author refers.

The problem is being tackled by use of persistent identifiers and schemes such as Handles, PURLs (Persistent URLs), and DOIs (Digital Object Identifiers). If such an identifier is available, use it when citing online references.

Accessing other sources of information

Grey literature

British Library

The British Library holds British reports, doctoral theses, and conference publications[20] which can be searched using the integrated catalogue.

GreySource

GreySource[21] is an online resource provides links to sources of grey literature. It is arranged by broad subject headings.

Theses and dissertations

Doctoral theses are usually available to anybody who wishes to read them (although some have restricted access owing to sensitive content). Some confidential works may be accessed with special permission from the author or other persons. In the UK doctoral theses not supplied by the home institution can be accessed via the British Library's British Thesis Service.[22] The item will be supplied in microform. If the British Library does not hold the full text, there will be a delay while they obtain the original document for microfilming from the originating institution. However, a new online UK thesis service will replace the existing service in the near future. Obtaining the hardcopy full text of items from overseas may be difficult, or at the very least, take some time.

Electronic Theses and Dissertations (ETD)

Increasing numbers of higher education institutions are providing full text open access to their own theses and dissertations electronically, although the UK has lagged behind developments in the US and Australia. As more institutional repositories are created and filled, more theses are becoming freely available online and the new national service, EThOS, will make UK theses much more easily available and accessible.

Networked Digital Library of Theses and Dissertations (NDLTD)[23]

This repository has members mainly in the US, but also from Canada, the UK, and other countries. Information about items is provided by member institutions, or submitted by their authors, and results in a union catalogue of ETDs.

Australasian Digital Theses (ADT)

The Australasian Digital Theses Program[24] is an online collection of digital postgraduate research theses awarded by Australian universities. It includes entries of research theses (PhD and Masters by Research) with full bibliographic information, an abstract, and links to the full text. The member institutions are all Australian universities. Theses eligible for deposit are those passed by a participating institution.

Official publications

Official documents may include items such as government committee reports. The BOPCRIS database provides full text access to a limited number of documents, 1688–1995. More documents are being added as part of the digitization of eighteenth century parliamentary documents. The 19th Century House of Commons Parliamentary Papers (HCPP) is an online collection to which many HE institutions might subscribe.

OPSI (Office of Public Sector Information) (and HMSO (Her Majesty's Stationery Office)) 'provides a wide range of services to the public, information industry, government and the wider public sector relating to finding, using, sharing and trading information' (OPSI 2007) and provides online access to UK legislation, the IAR (Information Asset Register), command papers, *London*, *Edinburgh*, and *Belfast Gazettes* (full access is a subscription service).

The National Archives (TNA) service provides access to digitized public records. Although searching is free: having found a reference many items can be viewed by visiting TNA or can be sent to the researcher for a fee. Not all downloading of images is free.

Datasets

Many datasets require a subscription, particularly maps and spatial data. Others such as the UK Data Archive (UKDA)[25] provides free access to digital data in the social sciences and humanities to anyone in UK HE. It also incorporates other data services such as Qualidata (social science qualitative datasets).

UK National Statistics provides free online access to many economic and socio-economic time series data sets, statistics, and National Statistics publications.

The National Geophysical Data Center[26] provides links to world data centres in the areas of geography, glaciology, geology, geophysics, and so on. Specialist knowledge may be needed for access to the correct data in a useable format.

Conference literature

Conference proceedings and pre-prints are often published by the society or academic body which organized the conference and may be available via that body for a charge. Many conference proceedings are made available on the WWW, some free and some as a charged service. Increasingly such items may be available via institutional repositories. The British Library provides access to conference publications that it holds in its Conference Collections.[27]

Standards and patents

Many large libraries stock standards and patents relevant to their users either in print or online. The status of items (whether they are current or have been superseded) can be checked using online services.

Images and sound

Institutions may subscribe to collections of images such as the Education Image Gallery and Education Media OnLine[28] hosted by Edina. Another service is the National Sound Archive from the British Library.[29] Materials will not necessarily be stored in a digital format.

Archives

Accessing archive materials such as local history, council, genealogical, or planning records could take some dedication as the only available source may be the original copy. Once the item has been located, the user may have to make a special journey to access it.

Company information

It can be difficult to find the details and to access reports or marketing information from industry. Much of this information is either commercially sensitive or not in the public domain. Libraries might hold marketing information such as that published by Mintel or a company reports database. Such information is usually expensive. Business libraries can provide extensive company and business information but users should check permissions for access before visiting such libraries.

Key points

- Leave enough time to find a means of accessing items not available immediately at the home library
- Explore all possibilities of accessing materials from the home institution including reciprocal access and borrowing schemes
- Check open access availability

Checklist

1   Have you checked what is easily available at your home institution?
2   Can you access items that you require freely on the Internet using a reputable open access repository?
3   What other resources will you need to use to access the information you require?
4   Will you need to order any items using interlibrary loan or other document supply service?

11

Evaluation of resources

The importance of evaluation • *Criteria for evaluation*

The importance of evaluation

Analysis of the problem and definition of the information need will have laid the foundations for the evaluation of resources. During the research process the researcher will encounter much more information than they will use, and they will have to select or reject what they find in order to build a relevant reserve for the project. The process of selection will be governed by evaluation. Any resource that is selected must have been chosen for its relevance: any that are irrelevant should be rejected.

The question, 'Is this resource relevant to the project?' should be considered for every item that is encountered. For some resources it is obvious they are irrelevant, but for others, it is not so straightforward.

The process of evaluation takes place throughout the research process as resources are discovered, located, and accessed. All types of resources should be evaluated for relevance, whatever their length or format, that is, whether it is the citation, abstract, or full text of a document, photograph, list of data, or government report.

Academics use a well respected method of evaluation called peer review. This is when articles or other items are scrutinized by expert reviewers prior to publication. This process often takes place using a blind review procedure or with the reviewers remaining anonymous to the author(s). Some disciplines or communities use the practice of open review where the item is made widely available for others to comment on it. Researchers should take trouble to find out whether they materials they wish to use have been peer reviewed or not. It is worth noting that open access journal articles have often been subject to as critical a peer review process as their closed access counterparts.

Practical considerations

Citations or bibliographic descriptions

Citations and bibliographic descriptions can be difficult to evaluate for relevance because so little information is included. Additional information may be required to judge some items. This could mean accessing publisher's information or obtaining the full text in order to facilitate a more informed decision.

Abstracts and summaries

Abstracts and summaries are excellent for assessing validity and relevance. They are short enough to be read quickly and, providing they are well written, include key points in a succinct and meaningful manner.

Full content

The researcher will not have the time or the inclination to read the entire content of every full text resource, such as books or articles, they encounter. They therefore have four options:

- To read any given abstract or summary. In the case of a book, this might be the introduction, the information on the back cover or that supplied by a publisher
- To read any headings or tables of contents
- To scan the document. This is a skill in itself and takes some practice
- To look carefully at any diagrams or tables that are included in the item as they give much information in an easily digested form

For many items, evaluation is a two stage process. If selected using, say, only a citation, the researcher should have the evaluation criteria in mind when reading the full text.

Criteria for evaluation

Like the evaluation of a website (see Chapter 9), there are a number of criteria that should be considered when attempting to evaluate a resource:

- Provenance: author, authority, reputation, publisher
- Content: level, composition, accuracy, comprehensiveness, currency, bias, substantiality, uniqueness, validity, intended audience, writing and language, organization

- Relation to the subject: importance of work, comparison with other sources
- Access and use: availability, accessibility, timescale, permissions, format

Table 11.1 lists questions that should be considered when evaluating a resource. The researcher should consider those that have some bearing on the item under scrutiny. A decision about relevance can be taken fairly quickly, depending on the responses. The entries in bold type are first step, quick check questions which will help the researcher check quickly whether a resource should be rejected or not.

Table 11.1 Evaluation of resources: points to consider

Provenance	
Author	**Who is the author?**
	What are the author's qualifications, reputation, or credentials?
	Does the author have any affiliation with a recognized body or institution?
	Is the author a recognized expert in the subject area?
	Is the author cited by other experts in the subject?
	If there is no named author(s), from where does the item originate?
Authority	**Has the resource been peer reviewed, refereed, or edited?**
	Has the resource been sponsored in any way or validated by a recognized authority (perhaps in a forward)?
	Are any references to the resource from reputable sources?
	Have the details been obtained from a reliable source?
Publisher	Is the publisher a recognized academic publisher or other recognized source?
	If not, what is their reputation?
Content	
Accuracy	**Where possible, check the accuracy of the content**
	Are spelling, diagrams, and typesetting accurate?
Bias	What is/are the reason(s) for publication? For example, extending knowledge or commercial?
	Is there any obvious or more subtle bias, political, commercial, or otherwise?
	Is there any evidence of commercial sponsorship?
Comparisons	Does the resource duplicate material from other sources?
	If so, which sources should be retained and which rejected?
	Does the author repeat material written by others?
	Does the resource include research methods or design similar to those being used by the researcher?
Composition	Are there any indexing terms, descriptors, keywords, or subject headings to describe the content?
	Is the resource a primary or secondary source?
Comprehensiveness	Have any topics or elements been omitted?
	Does the resource achieve its stated purpose?
	Does the content match the abstract or table of contents?
	Does the content meet the claims of the author or abstract?
	Is there too much/too little detail?
	Is the coverage too broad/too narrow?
	Does the research topic form the main topic or a peripheral topic?

Currency	**What is the date of publication?**
	There may be some time between conception and publication. Is the resource still valid?
	If the content is historical, is it relevant?
Intended audience	At whom is the resource mainly aimed?
	Is the level too simplistic/too complex?
Organization	Is the division of chapters and sections useful to the reader?
	Do any headings make sense?
	Do diagrams or illustrations enhance the text?
	Are diagrams, illustrations, and tables placed in close proximity to relevant text, avoiding awkward page turns?
	Is the title meaningful and does it reflect the content?
	Does the resource contain additional information such as further reading or information about related materials?
	Are the layout and typesetting clear and easy to use?
	Are sections an appropriate length for ease of use?
	Is the system of numbering or headings useful to the user?
	Is the index comprehensive
Substance	What is the tone of the content?
	Does it have seriousness and gravitas?
	Is it significant?
Uniqueness	Can the information be obtained elsewhere?
	Does the resource contain ground-breaking research or other original work?
	Is the resource a unique primary source?
Validity	**Is the work based on sound research?**
	Are references and a bibliography included?
	Are any citations from reputable sources?
	Is there reliable evidence to support any claims or results of investigations?
	Is any data used gathered from reliable sources?
Use of language	Are explanations clear?
	Is the sentence construction confused or too verbose?
	What is the style of writing: academic, informal?
	Is the text grammatically correct?
	Are any technical terms, acronyms, or other unusual terms explained?
Relation to the subject	
Comparisons	Does the content support or oppose other subject specialists?
Publication	If an article, what is the journal's impact factor rating?
Significance	**Is the resource a significant work in the subject area?**
	Have other respected authors in the subject field made reference to the work?
Access and use	
Availability	Does the complete item exist?
	If so, where?
Accessibility	**Is the content accessible by the researcher?**
	If it is accessible, is it available in time for the researcher's needs?
Format	Is the resource in a format that is acceptable to the researcher?
	Is it clear what the format will be (from bibliographic or descriptive details)?
	Is the resource available in multiple formats?

(*Continued overleaf*)

Table 11.1 Continued

	What is the country of origin of the resource? In what language is the full text (this may differ to the bibliographic details)? If the language is one not used by the researcher, is a translation available? Will the country of origin have any bearing on the content (for example, bias)
Permissions	**Is any special permission required to access or use the resource?** Can copyright and other permissions be obtained in time? Is it clear who should be contacted to obtain any permissions?
Overall judgement	**Does the resource comply with the criteria set when delimiting the area of research?**

Key points

- Every item should be tested with the question, 'Is this resource relevant to the project?'
- The evaluation can take the form of a serious of pertinent questions

Checklist

1   Are you satisfied that the information you have gathered or intend to gather satisfies your criteria in provenance, content, and relation to the subject?
2   Can you access and do you have permission to use the information you have found?

12

Citing references

Terminology • The purpose of citing references • Citation and reference style

Terminology

The following terms are often confused and sometimes used interchangeably:

- Citation: quotation of or inspiration derived from a passage, book, or author in support of an argument. The citation appears in the body of the text. All citations should be included in the list of references.
- References: a list of sources cited (referred to) in the text.
- Bibliography: a list of sources which may or may not be cited including other relevant or interesting sources, or a list of sources by a particular author or on a specified subject. A bibliography can be a discrete publication containing lists of works by a particular author or on a single subject and so on.
- Further reading: additional sources that may be of interest to the reader. It is used instead of, not as well as, a bibliography.
- Footnote: a note given at the foot of a page referring to something on that page. It is usually indicated by a figure or letter.
- Endnote: a note given at the end of a chapter or at the end of the text referring to something within that chapter or text. Endnotes are usually indicated by a figure or letter.

References to publications are used:

1 For citation searching and finding other articles of interest

2 When citing authors/publications in one's own work

The author should always give the citation of any work when it is referred to in the text. When composing references there are some points to note:

- There are a number of different styles of referencing (see below)
- The author should select the preferred style of any body or person for whom they are writing (such as a publisher or academic department)
- There are set elements of information that should be included
- Consistency is paramount
- The author should ensure that all punctuation and typefaces are correct
- The use of bibliographic software aids consistency and accuracy (see Chapter 13)

The purpose of citing references

Any work such as a doctoral thesis, a report, or an article is likely to have been influenced by the work of others, building on existing knowledge to form new arguments or to critique or compare views. Some require a review of the literature in order to:

- Demonstrate knowledge and an understanding of the subject
- Demonstrate an awareness of works and authors that have been instrumental in the development of, or provide meaningful comment on, the subject
- Provide a framework for the remainder of the dissertation or thesis

Other pieces of work can be primarily vehicles to demonstrate knowledge or are a résumé of the subject.

Whatever the case, the researcher should give full acknowledgement to the works or ideas of others referred to in the text:

1 So that the reader is assured that the work is based on or influenced by other reputable work
2 So that the reader can follow up any references of interest
3 As evidence of other's work that has been used to formulate the conclusions
4 To avoid unsubstantiated claims
5 To acknowledge the work of others
6 To avoid plagiarism (see Chapter 14)

Citation and reference style

The main consideration with style is to be consistent. Once a style has been selected, the author should adhere to it unfailingly. Care should be taken with accuracy of referencing, both the information included and how it is presented.

The author should check any existing guidelines and take care to follow them if writing as part of an award bearing course, for a publisher or a conference paper, or in any other situation.

Citing within the text

Citations within the text may be a passing reference or a direct quotation from an author. They may focus on either the author or the idea (Sharp et al. 2002: 202).

* Focus on the author: Fleming (1928) proved that . . .
* Focus on the idea: the staphylococci are unable to grow because of the presence of the mould (Fleming 1928)

Elements of a reference

A reference has fixed elements (BSI 1989: 3) which should be included for accuracy and fullness of information. The elements vary according to the format of the work or item being referenced but can be universally expressed by the following:

* Originator: author, artist, composer, editor, inventor, official body, or organization
* Date of publication or creation
* Title of the individual item: a book, article, Web page, and so on
* Place of origin
* Publisher/owner
* Format (when necessary)
* New version or replacement information: edition number, revised version, and in the case of Web pages, the date it was accessed
* Identifier or number: volume and issue number, number in a series, URL, page number(s)
* Title of work or series in which the item is contained: title of the journal, title of book or map series

Other elements might also be included depending on the item being referenced, such as the scale of a map, the language used for a computer program, or details of a foreign language or translation.

How to obtain the information to be included

The information included in the reference should be obtained directly from the item, for example, the reverse of the title page of a book or on any container. Other sources might include publisher's materials or other catalogues. If there are any inconsistencies in the information given (for example between the front cover and the title page), then the most prominent instance should be used (unless it is obviously incorrect).

Style

There are numerous styles of referencing, the two most common being Harvard and numeric (or Vancouver). As far as the author is concerned, the main advantage of using a style such as Harvard is that it is easier to manage when making amendments to the text, because the order of the list of references does not change (they are alphabetical rather than in the order that they appear in the body text). Others prefer numeric styles for being less intrusive in the text.

Even within a set style, there are variants such as use of bold text, italics, or underlining to highlight an element, differences in capitalization, or the exact punctuation used. Information given on how to cite references should be considered as guidance, and the author should use their discretion for the exact details. However, some publishers or organizations expect precise styles. Authors should consult guidance on citation styles that have been supplied before submitting a manuscript.

British Standard 5605: 1990 provides some guidance on how to apply the principles of citing and referencing (BSI 1990).

Harvard method

The Harvard method of citing is when the citations are placed within the text. The citation should include the surname of the author being quoted or referred to and the year of the publication being cited. For example:

• (Rumsey 2007)

If the author's name appears in the body text, the year is given in brackets. For example:

• Rumsey (2007) suggests that . . .

Depending on the selected style, page numbers may be included. For example:

• Rumsey (2007: 11–13)

References by the same author written in the same year, should append an extra letter: a, b, and so on. For example, Rumsey (1999a) and Rumsey (1999b). These letters should also be included in the reference list.

The references are then listed at the end of the document, in alphabetical order of author in the preferred style. For example, a reference for the first edition of this book might be constructed as follows:

RUMSEY, S. (2004). *How to find information: a guide for researchers*. Maidenhead: Open University Press

Or it could be in a different style:

Rumsey, Sally. *How to find information: a guide for researchers*. Maidenhead: Open University Press, 2004.

Styles can vary by discipline or professional body. Some in common use are those used by the IEEE, the APA, and the MLA (Modern Languages Association).

Numeric or Vancouver method

The numeric method operates by each citation being allotted a number in sequence. In this way, the first citation the reader encounters in a document is number one, the second number two, and so on. The list of references is therefore created using the order that the citations appear in the text. If a citation is used a second or subsequent time, it is assigned the original number. The number of the citation in the text may be given in brackets or superscript, for example:

- The school of thought that Freud [23] developed was . . .
- The school of thought that Freud[23] developed was . . .

In the list of references, the author's name may be given in the order: first name, last name rather than the other way round because the reader finds the reference using the allotted numbers, not the name.

Footnotes and endnotes

A method that is generally less common is that of incorporating references as footnotes. However, the legal community uses this method and, in addition, often gathers together the cases cited in a text in a list at the end. It can be argued that the use of footnotes is intrusive to the flow of the text. The footnote appears at the bottom of the page on which it is mentioned.

Electronic resources and other formats

Items other than books or journal articles can prove difficult to reference, particularly government publications and electronic resources such as websites. Each set style usually offers guidance in this area but that often does not solve queries such as defining the author of a website. There are numerous models for citing electronic resources such as those listed by IFLA (International Federation of Library Associations and Institutions; IFLA 2005).

Citing References: A Guide for Users (Fisher and Hanstock 2003) gives the following model for citing websites in Harvard format:

> AUTHOR or EDITOR, year. Title [online]. Place of publication: Publisher. Available at: <URL> [Accessed Date].

The author can be the same as the publisher who may be a large organization. It is important not to be confused between the author/publisher (who creates the intellectual content of the site) and the webmaster (who is concerned with the technical maintenance of the site). If page numbers are not given on the resource, then they cannot be included in the reference (although paragraph or chapter numbers may be an alternative if included in the text).

The URL of the resource should be included and the date it was accessed and enough detail given for any reader to find the item (providing it is still in existence). For any problematic item, the writer should remain consistent and refer to any guidelines that are appropriate such as those provided by Fisher and Hanstock, any other suitable guide or a relevant professional body.

Complex problems

The basis of citing and referencing sources is logical and straightforward, it is merely a question of using the correct data in the correct order in the specified form. However, many sources present an author with problems of how to cite them. The electronic resources above are a case in point.

Problems which often arise are:

- Difficulties in ascertaining the correct details about an item
- Using references from other sources where the cited work has not been read or accessed – only the citation has been read
- Using material from other formats such as maps, films and official documents, and non-standard materials

An author should do their utmost to find the correct details about an item. This may require using other sources such as other libraries' catalogues or publisher catalogues to check details. Use of square brackets may be made to indicate information supplied by the person citing the reference or information added for clarification. British Standard 1629: 1989 (BSI 1629: 1989) provides helpful points on difficulties such as these.

Making use of any guidelines including those mentioned in this chapter should help with other difficulties. A supervisor, librarian, or other information professional may be able to provide help.

Abbreviations of titles

Within references, accepted abbreviations are often used for the titles of journals or other publications. These should only be used if they are accepted by the publication and authors should take care that they use the correct abbreviation as some publications use the same letters, or similar abbreviations can easily be confused. For example, JCB can be used for:

- *Journal of Commercial Bank Lending*
- *Journal of Contemporary Business*
- *Journal of Creative Behavior*
- *Jurisprudence Commerciale de Bruxelles*
- *Kansas Judicial Council Bulletin*

Similar abbreviations:

- Ann Biol   *Annales Biologiques*
- Ann Biol An   *Annales de Biologie Animale, Biochimie,*
                          et Biophysique
- Ann Biol Cl   *Annales de Biologie Clinique* (Paris)
- Ann Biol (Copenhagen)   *Annales Biologiques* (Copenhagen)

(taken from *Periodical Title Abbreviations*, Alkire 2006)

A publication such as *Periodical Title Abbreviations* should be used to find accepted abbreviations (Alkire 2006).

Legal journals and law reports use abbreviations extensively. There are publications dedicated to listing legal abbreviations including Raistrick's book (Raistrick 1993) and Cardiff University Law Library's online database (Information Services, Cardiff University, 2004).

Other abbreviations

Other abbreviations that might be encountered are as follows:

- Ibid. (itself an abbreviation of ibidem and sometimes further abbreviated to ib.) means 'in the same book or passage' (as the one quoted immediately before it). Often confused with op. cit. (see below)

- Op. cit. (opere citato) means 'in the work already quoted' and refers the reader to a previous citation. It is therefore necessary to include the author's name in the citation.
- Et al. (et allii: and others) generally used when an item has three or more authors or creators

---

Key points

- Always reference a work when it is cited in the text, whether quoted directly or as a passing reference
- Be consistent in reference style
- Use the correct style for the situation
- Make sure the content and the typesetting of the references is accurate

---

Checklist

1   What style of referencing are you using? Why?
2   Have you referenced every work you have cited?
3   Will you include a list of works of further interest to your readers which you haven't actually cited?
4   Do you have the full details of all the references you cite?
5   Is your referencing consistent? Have you consistently used the correct typeface and punctuation?
6   Have you identified a source of help for referencing queries (librarian, academic, reference work, etc.)?
7   Are you using bibliographic software (see Chapter 13)?

13

Keeping records

Efficient searching and well ordered records • Maintaining records of searches • Saving records and details of works accessed • Bibliographic software

Efficient searching and well ordered records

Earlier chapters advocate the need for organized preparation and information seeking. Well ordered records and processes make the management and use of information a straightforward and painless process. There will be occasions when incomplete records or other problems arise, but if the researcher is able to start from a logically constructed and managed base, the whole process should save time, wasted effort, and frustration.

The complexity and methods of information storage and record keeping will depend largely on the size of the project. It might not be worth spending time (and possibly money) setting up a complex bibliographic software system for a short piece of work. For a large scale project such as a doctoral thesis, bibliographic software would be invaluable, especially if undertaken at the outset of the work.

Maintaining records of searches

The researcher who has prepared their search strategy (see Chapter 6) will have records of the searches they intend to run. The results of those searches and follow-up tactics resulting from the success or otherwise may differ from the original plan:

- Some searches may have produced too few or too many results
- Alternative terms may have been discovered prompting additional searches
- The searcher may have access to additional resources, for example, if the library subscribes to a new database

In order to ensure that the researcher does not waste time re-running searches already performed, or is able to check back and re-run previously run searches to gather updates, records of searches should be maintained.

To do this there are a number of options, including written and electronic solutions. Some may like to jot down the searches carried out and the results in a notebook or other safe place. Others might prefer an electronic solution such as a word processed document, spreadsheet, or database. The advantages of electronic solutions are that records can be sorted for ease of reference and the results printed out if required, perhaps as part of an assessed assignment. Whatever the format, the information will include:

- search terms
- source (such as the name of the database or index used)
- date on which the search was run (or edited)
- numbers of results
- relevance of results
- notes for future searches
- numbering of each search for ease (if using a database, this may be essential)

For example, an entry in a search log for a researcher working in the topic area of perception and the developing child may include entries such as those in Table 13.1.

Printouts of search histories (see below) may be adequate, but additional information such as the date the search was run should be added.

Saving searches and search histories

The search history created when running searches on a database can be printed out for reference. As mentioned in Chapter 5, some online databases allow the user to save their searches and search histories for later reference or editing during a future session.

Saving records and details of works accessed

Saving individual records is vital for:

- Creating a complete reference list and for citing references

Table 13.1 Example of a word processed record of searches

No.	Search terms	Source	Date	Limits	Nos. of results	Relevance	Notes
1	(Infant or child* or toddler or baby or babies) AND (perception OR perceive)	Web of Knowledge	15.6.07	L = English J	5471	Mixed	Needs refining. Meaning of word perception
2	(aural OR audio) AND (perception OR perceive)	Web of Knowledge	15.6.07	L = English J	281	High	
3	(Infant or child* or toddler or baby or babies) AND (perception OR perceive)	PsycINFO	20.6.07	D = from 1990 L = English J	386	Mixed	Needs refining. Meaning of word perception
4	(aural OR audio) AND (perception OR perceive)	PsycINFO	20.6.07	D = from 1990 L = English J	18	High	Some language references
5	aural perception	ZETOC	19.1.07	None	18	High	
6	Author name: Hollier M P	Ingenta	19.1.07	None	5	High	

Notes: D = date of publication; L = language; J = journal articles.

- Following up references
- Creating a databank of references in a particular subject for future use

Many online databases allow the user to save, print, or download records (see Chapter 5).

Whatever the task, the researcher should keep full and accurate records of works and bibliographic records that have been accessed. A hastily scribbled quotation or a photocopied page that does not contain work details is often impossible to track down later on. Another trap is that of noting the author and title of a chapter that forms a chapter of a book, but failing to keep a record of the editor and title of the book itself.

All too often it is when the work is drawing to a close and a deadline is looming that the researcher realizes they do not have the full details for the list of references. Panic then ensues, and they either have to hope that luck prevails or that the item in question can be recovered using an electronic search. If a reference cannot be traced, they may have to remove it.

Bibliographic software

Bibliographic software (or reference management software) is designed to allow users to store, manage, and use references. There are a number of commercial systems on the market and many academic establishments provide use of one or more packages for their members. There are also some open source products in development.

The software provides functions such as:

- Allowing the user to download references directly to the database from some (but not all) bibliographic databases such as Web of Knowledge. Note that the exported references should be checked carefully to ensure they are accurate and consistent
- Manipulation of the data in order to format the references into the correct bibliographic style (such as Harvard or that of a specific journal or publisher)
- Automated linking of the citation in the text with the reference at the end
- Enabling easy creation and formatting of a list of references
- Providing a means of building a personal library of references

Setting up the software to one's personal preferences requires time and skill. Therefore, it is advisable to use this software if the project warrants it or if the user intends to continue to build a personal library beyond the project. Once it has been set up, it is straightforward to run and can save much time and effort. Creating the list of references in this way also eliminates errors in formatting such as incorrect punctuation or typographical errors when re-typing (providing, of course, that the formatting is set up correctly and the original text bears no mistakes). It is also a convenient means of storing a large collection of references.

For those online bibliographic databases that are set up to import references to bibliographic software, the process of adding references is quick and straightforward. For some, it is necessary to deal with filters which can be a complex issue and users should read the product's instructions carefully. Many academic libraries provide training for their students in how to use bibliographic software. However, not all online bibliographic databases are designed to enable the user to download references directly into a bibliographic software package. There may be an option to save the results as a text file which can then be imported into the bibliographic database. The imported references may need some editing.

Some packages are available for PDA (Personal Digital Assistant) computers (and, of course, can be used on laptops) which researchers may find useful when roaming. Being able to add references, even manually, while on the move can enable more accurate and up to date collections.

Using bibliographic software

Use of this software means that if you use one style of referencing in one document, you can easily change the style of the same references when writing another document which saves considerable time and effort. References can be added manually or can be downloaded from some bibliographic databases or catalogues (see above). As with all software, it is only as good as the information entered. Therefore it is important that data are entered correctly, particularly when entering them manually. It is necessary to ensure that information is entered in the correct format, for example, that an author's name is entered with the elements in the correct order and with the correct punctuation or spacing, otherwise it will not be indexed correctly. Check the usage instructions of the software you are using. Be particularly careful when including titles, double-barrelled names, and names of institutions that they display correctly.

Users can create separate sets of references (sometimes called libraries). It is possible to add personal keywords to stored references for ease of use (for example, to indicate all the references on a particular topic). Bibliographic software packages usually contain many pre-set styles of referencing, for example as used in particular journals or by well known associations. It is also possible to create other styles. This is most easily achieved by editing a pre-set style which most closely matches the required style.

Using the citing within the text function on the software means that as citations are inserted in the text, the list of references is automatically built in the selected style. It may also be possible to create the references as footnotes instead of as a separate list.

Other means of keeping records of bibliographic details

Other options for managing references are given below. The time necessary for typing the references with the correct punctuation can be considerable and there is always the likelihood of error. It also takes time to compile the list of references, and any changes to the citations in the text have to be dealt with manually.

Social Web services

There are a number of free Web-based services which enable users to keep records of their libraries. One which is aimed at the academic community is Citeulike.[1] This service has an easy to use bookmarking feature which enables users to keep track of articles and papers of interest to them. Another example is Connotea where the user (it is aimed at clinicians and scientists) can store references by 'saving a link to a web page for the reference' (Connotea 2007). Bibliographic details for items are pulled in from sites such as PubMed and the user can add personal tags. The user can share their references with others. Personal libraries can be shared and users are able to tag items. LibraryThing[2] is an example of a personal online library catalogue which can then be shared with other users. There are other free general bookmark management Web services.

Such services can be of great use, are simple to set up, and free, but by their nature are not formally supported.

Word processing packages

References can be added into a word processing file using the method of saving the references as a text file as above. The references will probably need to be edited to create the correct style. The user should be assiduous when managing the stored information. Options include creating a new text document for each new library of references or retaining a master document of all references which can then be searched using the usual search/find function of the software in use. If the references are stored in a table format, the software may have a function to allow them to be sorted into alphabetical or numerical order.

Databases

It is possible to build a personal bibliographic database using database software. The complexity and functionality of such an imitation off the shelf bibliographic reference management file relies on the user's time and competence. A simple solution would be to create a database using basic fields (author, title, date, and so on) and then to create a bibliography or list of references using the report function of the database. The researcher would have to balance the time and effort of creating a personal version.

Cards and files

It is possible to build a reference library using a printed or written card index or file. Hand writing such entries is time consuming and does not offer the flexibility of cutting and pasting the details into the final document. It can, however, be convenient when working away from one's desk.

Key points

- Be assiduous in keeping records of searches, the relevant records retrieved and of any works accessed
- Save searches for reference and later updating
- Use reference management software if available and if the work warrants it

---

Checklist

1   How will you save a record of your searches?
2   Do you have the *full* details of all sources used?
3   If you have any photocopied extracts of works which you are intending to cite, do you have details of the work from which they were taken?
4   If you are using references taken from a chapter have you recorded the details of the book in which the chapter is included?
5   Do you wish to make use of bibliographic software?

14

Intellectual property and plagiarism

Introduction • Intellectual property • IP considerations when researching and creating documents • The IP of the researcher's work • Plagiarism

Introduction

The law regarding intellectual property is likely to affect anyone who is considering using other's work to influence their own work or who wishes to reproduce text, images, or other creations whether in hard copy or electronically. The researcher should therefore be aware of how they may be affected so that they can (1) remain within the law and (2) not commit academic malpractice, even unwittingly. Ignorance is no defence in this area. Conversely, the researcher (or their institution) may be entitled to obtain rights for their work.

Intellectual property

Intellectual property (IP) law exists in order to protect ideas and creative work from misuse and to allow the creator to gain rewards from their innovations and work. Intellectual property comprises four parts, one of which is copyright. Copyright is likely to be the area that affects the researcher most frequently. The four parts are:

- copyright
- patents
- trade marks
- designs

The law differs from country to country, although the EU is attempting to standardize regulations within its jurisdiction. There have been moves towards international agreements by WIPO (World Intellectual Property Organization) which is promoting the protection of intellectual property rights in a global context for its member states. In the UK it is the UK Intellectual Property Office or UK-IPO (formerly known as the Patent Office) that is responsible for IP. The UK statute concerned with this area over recent years has been the Copyright, Designs and Patents Act 1988, although a number of amendments have been introduced since it was first enforced.

Copyright

Copyright protection does not have to be applied for in the same way as other IP rights. It comes into effect automatically and immediately the work is created in a physical form: on paper, film, and so on. It is the work that is protected, not the idea behind that work. The medium of the work may be physical or electronic: all media are protected by copyright.

The UK-IPO lists the types of works that copyright protects as:

- 'Computing and the internet: Copyright applies to computing and the internet in the same way as material in other media'. It includes downloads, uploads, databases, and computer programs.
- Photographs: 'Photographs, digital or on film, are protected by copyright as artistic works. The exact rules relating to copyright in photographs vary according to the law which was in place at the time the photograph was taken'.
- TV and films: 'For TV productions and films, copyright may exist on a number of its components, for example, the original screenplay, the music score and so on'.
- Art: 'Copyright applies to original artistic works such as paintings, drawings, engravings, sculptures, photographs, diagrams, maps, works of architecture and works of artistic craftsmanship'.
- Written work: 'Copyright applies to original written work such as novels, newspaper articles, lyrics for songs, instruction manuals and so on. These are known as literary works. Copyright in a literary work lasts for the life of the author plus 70 years'.
- Music: 'Copyright applies to music when it is recorded, either by writing it down or in any other manner. With a song there will usually be more than one copyright associated with it'.

- Theatre: 'Copyright applies to any original live theatrical performance such as ballet, opera, plays, musicals, pantomimes and so on'.
- Spoken word: 'There is no copyright in speech unless and until it is recorded'. Performers 'may be entitled to performer's rights'.

The Text above is quoted from UK IPO copyright information at www.ipo.gov.uk/copy.htm

It should be noted that copyright covers works available on the Internet. A common misconception is that because a work is freely available via the Internet, it is available to be downloaded and used in any way the user wishes. This is not necessarily the case, and researchers should take care with such material to acknowledge and reference sources, gaining permission where necessary.

It is likely that in the course of information seeking and discovery, a researcher will wish to photocopy works or extracts from works. There are usually guidelines posted near photocopying machines that give details of what may or may not be legally copied.

The Copyright Licensing Agency (CLA) deals in licences for bodies such as academic institutions and the public service sector. Such licences are designed to enable copying that respects both the needs of creators and publishers, and those of the users. The CLA covers books, journals, magazines, and periodicals, but does not include all publications. Some works are excluded from licences arranged with the CLA, for example, maps, printed music, and all newspapers plus some publishers (CLA 2007). Copying under the fair dealing agreement allows additional copying under specified conditions, although this may change, and those wishing to copy should always check that what they intend complies with any licences and the law.

The photocopying bug can be addictive and researchers may find themselves copying anything that is vaguely relevant in case it may be useful. This, of course, costs money and the act of copying does not mean that the information will be learnt by a process of osmosis. Depending on the circumstances and the time available, it can be more beneficial to resort to the practice of note-taking or writing a précis. This can ensure that the researcher understands the work. Care must be taken to retain all reference information.

Libraries will probably answer copyright queries concerning the deposition of materials in an institutional repository. Many publishers allow works, both pre-prints and post-prints, to be deposited in this way. A useful source is the SHERPA/Romeo[1] website which summarizes current policies for many journal publishers, although users should be prepared to check the actual policy as given by the publisher in question.

A copyright balancing act

The balance between providing access to information and protecting the rights of creators is a difficult one that is constantly under discussion. The two sides are the information creators (who wish to certify themselves as creator of the work, disseminate their work, and add it to the research corpus and (not always) reap financial rewards), publishers (who wish to benefit financially from the publication), and information users who would often like information to be freely available. Piracy and commercial misuse hampers industry and further development, but use for educational and private use is often acceptable within limits. Difficulties have been encountered when attempting to agree what is fair use and what may be used without payment or permission. If in any doubt, anyone wishing to use copyrighted information should contact the rights holder for permission.

Changes in copyright law

There has been much discussion regarding Directive 2001/29/EC of the European Parliament and of the Council of 22 May 2001 on the harmonization of certain aspects of copyright and related rights in the information society. This directive was supposed to have been implemented by member states by December 2002, but in many countries this has not been the case. Fair dealing is one of the areas causing contention in the new directive. One change that users may have noticed is that of the period of time in which a work remains in copyright which was extended in the UK from 50 to 70 years in order to comply with the EU. This has caused some confusion, as works which had at one stage been out of copyright for some time, were then protected again. Researchers should be able to find advice regarding copyright from libraries and the UK-IPO.[2]

Researchers should make sure that they comply with current copyright law when copying, downloading, and using materials.

Patents

If an invention can fulfil the criteria of being new, involving an inventive step, being capable of industrial application, and not being excluded from certain defined categories, the inventor may apply for, and be granted, a patent. This can then be used to protect their invention from being made, used, or sold without the permission of the inventor for a set period of time. UK patents are only applicable within the UK. It is possible to obtain European or international patents for more extensive coverage. Those working in industrial or academic research may wish to apply for patents for their inventions. Full details for the UK may be obtained from the UK-IPO.

Trademarks

The UK-IPO describes a trade mark as 'any sign or symbol that allows your customers to tell you apart from your competitors' (UK-IPO 2003b). A trademark could be 'a name, logo, slogan, domain name, shape, colour or sound' (UK-IPO 2003b). They are used for easy recognition by the general public or others. Unauthorized use of these symbols can be a prosecutable offence.

If a researcher is considering developing a trade mark, they should seek advice on registration and other issues. Information is available from the UK-IPO.

International patents can be registered with countries which have signed the Madrid Protocol (see the WIPO[3] website) and European Community trademark information can be obtained from the Office for Harmonization of the Internal Market website.

Designs

The UK-IPO is the body in the UK that registers designs covering the 'outward appearance of your product, including decoration, lines, contours, colours, shape, texture and materials' (UK-IPO 2003c).

IP considerations when researching and creating documents

What is allowed?

For many, use of text will amount to the quotation or inclusion of short extracts or ideas which may be acknowledged in the references. If use of materials is not permitted by the rights holders, it is usually made abundantly clear on the item. Where it is not clear if permission is required, it is safest to err on the side of caution and contact the rights holders.

Obtaining permissions

Obtaining permissions can be a time consuming process and allowances for this should be planned.

It is important to remember that the rights holder and the author/creator may be different. This is often the case with images. If wishing to use any part or excerpt from a publication, check the acknowledgements which should give details of any permissions granted, so that the correct person is contacted in the first instance.

There are some items that are covered by collective management organization. These groups act on behalf of the rights owners by licensing copyright material where it is impractical for the rights owners to act as individuals. Such bodies include the MCPS (Mechanical Copyright Protection Society for the recording of music in any format), the PRS (Performing Rights Society for the public performance and broadcast of musical works) and the CLA (Copyright Licensing Agency) (for the reprographic reproduction of works, that is, photocopying).

Sometimes it is not possible to contact rights holders and where this is the case one sometimes finds words to the effect that every attempt to contact rights holders has been made and the authors would welcome any communication from those who could not be contacted.

Obtaining permissions for your thesis

It should be remembered that although material might be permitted to be included in a thesis for the purposes of examination, it does not automatically imply that the material may be made freely available via the Internet by the author of the thesis. This point needs to be considered by students whose final thesis will be made available electronically. It is recommended that researchers clear copyright permissions as they progress through their research so that as many materials as possible can be included for dissemination via the Internet in the final, freely available, online version. It also saves a lot of time and anguish when the thesis is submitted to the online repository or other system. If permission cannot be obtained for inclusion in the online version either the material will have to be removed or not made available to end-users.

The IP of the researcher's work

As stated above, copyright is automatically assigned to the physical manifestation of the researcher's work. This can be emphasized by marking the work with the copyright symbol (©), although this is not strictly necessary.

When submitting articles, papers, book manuscripts, and so on, the author should read any rights agreements carefully as they vary from publisher to publisher. Some publishers allow authors to retain the copyright of their work but sign over other publishing rights; others demand that the copyright of the work is signed over to the publisher; some may, for example, retain any publishing rights for a set period of time, after which all rights will revert back to the author. Some authors prefer to retain the rights to all their works and grant the publisher a licence to publish the works: 'it is not essential for publishers to acquire copyright in order to publish' (Gadd et al. 2003).

There are publishers that allow the author to retain copyright of their work: the author then grants the publisher a licence to publish. This licence can be exclusive or non-exclusive. Authors should be aware of their rights for all options and of the rights they retain to use their work after publication. Model addenda to copyright transfer agreements and other examples of alternative wording for authors to use in order to retain their rights in their work are available from bodies such as SPARC.[4] Authors should contact copyright and other legal experts for advice.

As well as the property rights included in copyright law, the author has certain moral rights which, unlike copyright, must be asserted by the author. A statement to this effect often appears on the verso of the title page of a book. An author's moral rights are:

- The right to be identified as the author
- The right to object to their name being associated with someone else's work
- The right not to have their work subjected to derogatory treatment

Authors are able to take legal proceedings if any of these rights are infringed.

The copyright of a thesis usually belongs to the author, but for a researcher employed by an institution or where there are other agreements, the institution may hold the copyright. Doctoral students and other researchers may find that any intellectual property included in their work is owned by their institution. This should be clarified before taking steps to use the information for any other purpose apart from their research.

As digital encryption and watermarking techniques improve and become more commonplace, authors and publishers of electronic materials may choose to incorporate these features into electronic publications and other electronic sources such as audio visual materials. Watermarking does not necessarily have the effect of preventing unlawful copying, but can authenticate a copy as being a legal copy or include information such as the rights holders' details. This will improve the security of the work as being that of the stated author (rather than someone else who claims it is their own) and can help prevent unlawful copying and misuse.

If it is appropriate, the researcher or their organization may choose to apply for a patent and/or register a design or trademark. Advice may be required from their institution, the UK-IPO or they may need to approach a third party such as a patent agent.

Creative Commons and licensing

The Creative Commons is devoted to providing a mechanism for the fair use of works. It has produced a set of freely available copyright licences. The corporation works 'to offer creators a best-of-both-worlds way to protect their works while encouraging certain uses of them' (Creative Commons 2007). A branch of the corporation, International Commons, is dedicated to jurisdictions other than the US. There are separate Creative Commons for England & Wales[5] and for Scotland.[6] Usage of the Creative Commons licences is growing, and with the addition of more countries, is set to become a standard method of dealing with rights at an international level.

The Creative Commons is running a project named Science Commons[7] to investigate the application of its philosophies and activities in the field of science.

Plagiarism

Academic institutions and others take plagiarism seriously and it is something that researchers and authors should take the trouble to be both aware of and avoid.

What is plagiarism?

Plagiarism can be defined as 'passing off someone else's work, intentionally or unintentionally, as your own, for your own benefit' (Carroll 2002), although there are differences in opinion and confusion in what constitutes plagiarism. It is, however, important to acknowledge all sources used.

One of the key words in the above definition is 'unintentionally'. This is where the researcher must be particularly alert and sensitive to possible occurrences of plagiarism when composing and checking their own work. Plagiarism can include:

- 'Copying a paragraph verbatim from a source without any acknowledgement'
- 'Copying a paragraph and making small changes – e.g., replacing a few verbs, replacing an adjective with a synonym; acknowledgement in the bibliography'
- 'Cutting and pasting a paragraph by using sentences of the original but omitting one or two and putting one or two in a different order, no quotation marks; with an in-text acknowledgement plus bibliography' (Carroll 2003)

Not only can plagiarism relate to the actual words written by an author, but also to their ideas. A researcher should be careful to acknowledge anything they produce that uses work previously carried out by another, whether its the words, the ideas behind the arguments, the diagrams, or any other parts of their work.

All sources should be correctly cited and referenced (see Chapter 12). The researcher should keep impeccable records of their sources of information so that they can check that nothing has been plagiarized and have full details of their sources to include in the list of references.

Software is being developed to aid detection of plagiarized material and a sure way of losing (at the very least) respect in academic circles is to use other's material without acknowledgement. However, most researchers do not need reminding that it is good practice and courteous to acknowledge the work of others.

Tips to help avoid plagiarism

Some useful tips to help avoid plagiarism are to:

- Copy direct quotes verbatim to ensure they have not been altered in any way
- Be clear when note-taking to include details of the author and source
- Become familiar with methods of citing within the text
- Only include passages vital to the argument
- Record one's own views and thoughts before beginning to find information, then use work by others to support or counter these arguments
- Be selective and do not include too many quotations
- Be careful when paraphrasing that the material is used properly
- Write notes from memory after reading the source

Anti-plagiarism software

Anti-plagiarism software is being used increasingly to both detect and deter plagiarism. Such software checks items against others and gives a report on how original the work is. There are a number of products on the market.

The JISC provides a Plagiarism Advisory Service (JISC PAS),[8] based on Turnitin software, to academic institutions, academics, and students, which includes the use of plagiarism detection software. The software can be used by students to check their own work prior to submission to the tutor. The 'Resources' section of the JISC PAS website gives many tips on how to avoid plagiarism.

Sanctions

Any sanctions resulting from plagiarism will depend upon the circumstances. In more minor cases, a warning may be given or, for academic work, marks may be deducted or an award withheld. For more serious cases, there may be legal implications.

For most, it is a case of educating authors before they fall foul of plagiarism and do not commit it unwittingly.

Key points

- Check the rights associated with any works being used
- Check the rights associated with any work being created
- Be aware of what constitutes plagiarism
- Become familiar with methods that help avoid plagiarism
- Acknowledge all sources

Checklist

1   Are you sure you have obtained permissions to use materials in which copyright is held by another party?
2   Have you acknowledged the copyright holder where relevant?
3   Will you want to use one of the Creative Commons or other licences for your work? If so, which one?
4   Have you read any copyright transfer agreement carefully and do you know what rights you have to use your work after submission to a publisher?
5   Do you wish to retain the copyright in your own work or grant an exclusive or non-exclusive licence to the publisher (if submitting to a publisher for publication)?
6   Are there any parts of your work for which you should apply for other IP protection, e.g., patent, design, etc.?
7   Can you be sure that you haven't plagiarized work by others?

15

The research community and keeping up to date

Introduction

Research can be a lonely pursuit: many hours spent working in a lab or office, reading and writing papers and reports in a highly specialist field with scholars scattered around the world. Conversely, the research community is a global and vibrant hive of activity, which a researcher can tap into easily using electronic communication. In such a fast moving world, it is vital to keep up to date with the latest developments and monitor work in similar settings. Many researchers thrive on contact with likeminded individuals. Achievements by others can become the inspiration for setting out along new and innovative pathways.

Keeping up to date partly means reading the latest issues of appropriate journals. However, there is a lot more that can be done and an active researcher will spend time mining for the most current and, often, unpublished materials. This chapter offers some suggestions for making contact with the research community and keeping abreast of developments.

The research community

Communication between researchers is vital for the dissemination of ideas and results. It is necessary to gather information and communicate with people in both the virtual and real worlds. The community comprises individuals, small groups, and large organizations which come together at certain points and in a variety of groupings. See Figure 15.1 for a diagrammatic representation of the research community.

Other institutions

A simple means of finding out about current activities is to access an institution's or research group's website. This may or may not include publications and reports of recent activities, but it can be a good starting point and can help identify the individuals or groups involved. They can be found via the HERO website, on some Intute subject websites, or by talking to others working in the same field.

Networking

Leaving a conference clutching a handful of business cards is a common occurrence. Having made the contacts it can be beneficial to keep records of who has been met, where they work, and the area in which they are involved before either losing the card or forgetting the detail. Building up a documented network can make the task of locating a person or a place where a specific topic is being researched that much easier. A simple database, spreadsheet, or notebook can suffice.

Many researchers become involved in the process of peer review for books or articles. This can be a valuable method of reading items of current interest.

COS and CORDIS

COS and CORDIS are examples of fora for finding details of other researchers and research partners for projects (see Chapter 3).

Intute

Each Intute[1] subject group provides services for researchers. MyIntute allows the user to set up a weekly email alerting service of new items added to Intute. There is also a conferences and events search for the social sciences.

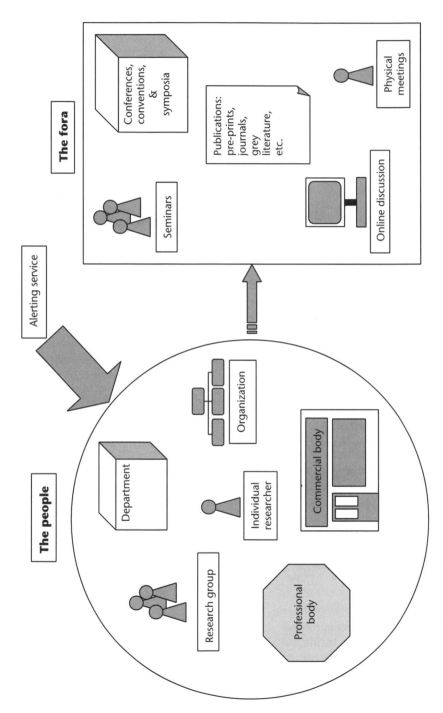

Figure 15.1 The research community

ISI Highly Cited

ISI Highly Cited forms part of the ISI Web of Knowledge service. It provides details of the most cited researchers (those included on the ISI citation databases) and is aiming to extend to the 250 most cited individuals in 21 broad subject categories in the areas of science, engineering, and social sciences. The information available includes biographical information and details of publications.

Scenta

SCENTA[2] is a portal for the science, engineering, and technology (SET) community. It provides the opportunity for users to find out about events and a discussion forum as well as links to resources.

Times Higher Education Supplement

The *Times Higher Education Supplement* (*THES*)[3] provides information about research funding opportunities (for online subscribers only) and conferences as well as news articles about higher education policy, individuals, and current debate. It is available in print and online.

Conferences, conventions, colloquia, and symposia

For the sake of ease, these headings will be referred to under the umbrella term 'conferences'. Gatherings of likeminded researchers are where researchers can discuss (and argue) current research activities with those directly involved. There are conferences in all subject areas. The difficulty can be in knowing about the conferences on offer. Many large conferences are planned many months or even years in advance. Anyone wishing to submit a paper has to work towards a deadline well ahead of the actual conference. Finding out what is happening on the conference circuit is an important aspect of a researcher's and organization's work. Conference discovery may take place by:

- reading journals
- being a member or obtaining details from a professional body
- accessing subject gateways
- a service such as Intute
- using a conferences dedicated website or directory
- a general Web search
- Web alerts or weblogs
- mailing/discussion lists

- talking to a colleague or other subject specialist
- print flyers

Conference directories

Many directories are Web-based and depend on the conference organizer submitting details to the site. Examples of Web-based multidisciplinary directories are AllConferences.com[4] or Conference Alerts.[5] Professional societies provide conference information both for their own institute and sometimes for external bodies. For example, the IEEE Ultrasonics, Ferroelectrics, and Frequency Control Society provides access to details of all IEEE conferences, and the Royal Historical Society lists conferences other than its own on its Web pages.

Alerting or current awareness services

So far, this chapter has been about gathering information about the research community and its current activities using action on the part of the researcher. There are many services that enable the researcher to set up sophisticated alerts so that information about publications, events, and other matters are automatically delivered to them electronically. These services are often referred to as current awareness or alerting services.

Databases

Most of the subscription online databases provide a facility to save one's searches (see Chapter 5). The user can open up a saved search on entering the database at a later time, to re-run and update it. This is often extended to being able to set up search alerts whereby the search will be automatically re-run at intervals and the user informed of any updates. The Elsevier Science Direct database provides an additional journal issue alert facility that notifies the user when a new issue of a selected journal becomes available on Science Direct. This database and also Scopus allows the setting up of citation alerts (see Chapter 7). Alert settings can be flexible, allowing the user to select frequency and format of delivery.

Publishers

Traditionally publishers have sent out their catalogues to interested parties to alert them to available publications and tempt them into purchasing copies. This practice is still flourishing but has disadvantages including the cost of the paper, printing and postage, the cost of duplication with outdated mailing lists, and irrelevancy because of the recipients being selected by the publisher. An electronic version can be more cost effective and easily managed. In addition, delivery and receipt of the information can be almost instantaneous.

Many of the major publishers such as Blackwells, Oxford University Press, and the Open University Press[6] offer email alerting services for information about new publications. The user is able to specify the subject area(s) of interest.

Official publications

For official publications in the UK, UKOP provides a weekly email alerting service and the Office of Public Sector Information (OPSI) provides RSS feeds for new legislation.

Tables of contents (ToC) services

Tables of contents alerts are particularly useful as the user is made aware of all the items within a particular publication. This means that, although they will be alerted to some articles which are of no interest, there may be items about related subjects that would not have been selected by a keyword search.

Zetoc

For those eligible to use Zetoc, alerts by email or RSS feeds can be set up to inform the user of tables of contents of publications as they are added to the vast collection of the British Library's Tables of Contents of journals and conference proceedings. The user may set up multiple alerts using one or more titles.

Databases such as those provided by CSA Illumina can be set up for ToC alerting. This can be achieved by running a search using one or more sources (using a journal title or ISSN) then saving the search as an alert. New additions to the results will then be sent automatically to the subscriber.

Journal publishers such as Sage,[7] OUP,[8] and Springer[9] provide a table of contents alerting service. The recipient may receive information about forthcoming articles and papers in advance of publication. The Springer Keyword alerts service allows the user to submit keywords as the basis for an altering service. InformaWorld[10] from Taylor & Francis (T&F) provides an alerting service for T&F publications which comprises a number of different types of alerts. There is also an RSS feed facility for subject or publication alerts.

Commercial document supply services such as InfoTrieve[11] sometimes offer a table of contents alerting service to which the user can subscribe by setting up their own profile.

Research news

Research news is made available via a number of sources: professional bodies, charities, and academic departments. Other fora such as EurekAlert from the American Association for the Advancement of Science (AAAS)[12] enable researchers to post news about their work which can then be accessed by others. These initiatives rely on submission of items by researchers or their institutions.

Mailing/discussion lists

Mailing lists are a means of monitoring current topics of interest and taking part in discussion with others working in a similar field. There is a danger in joining too many lists and becoming inundated with emails. There are lists in most disciplines, varying from the general to the highly specific. The activity of the lists varies from those where subscribers may receive many messages each day to those which lie dormant for long periods. Surveying the archives gives the user a feel for the amount of activity on any list. Fortunately, there are means by which a user's subscription can be suspended during times of inactivity such as during vacations, so that on return there are not hundreds of new emails waiting.

Although many lists are open to all, some are closed, that is, available only to those complying with specific criteria (for example, those for heads of departments). Lists are monitored by a list manager who steps in if the service is being abused or irrelevant messages posted.

In UK higher and further education circles there are many lists sponsored by the JISC in the Jiscmail[13] national academic mailing list service. There is no cost to the list subscriber or the list manager for these lists. Globally there are numerous lists in existence that run using the commercial LISTSERV[14]software. It is possible to search for lists that use this system using the company's own Catalist search engine service.

Web 2.0

There are a multitude of blogs and wikis aimed at keeping researchers in touch with current developments. Many are provided by individuals and so the user should be careful to evaluate the quality and authority when assessing the content. That said, such methods of communication can be invaluable.

Key points

- Find ways of contacting and monitoring other researchers, research groups, and institutions
- Keep up with conference activity in the selected subject area
- Set up alerts to stay informed of new publications
- Join a mailing list to monitor current developments and to contact those working in similar subjects

Checklist

1   Have you signed up for relevant alerts?
2   Are there any useful discussion lists in your subject area?
3   How will you find out about conferences and events that are relevant to you?
4   How best can you keep informed about current developments in your subject?

16

The changing landscape of research

Introduction • JISC activities • Dissemination of research results
• Searching for research materials • Open URLs • e-Books and e-theses
• The importance of data • The e-Science programme and the Grid
• Means of managing and presenting information • Digital preservation
and curation • Research Information Network (RIN) • Journal impact
factors, peer review, and citation services

Introduction

The combination of improving research support in libraries, increasing numbers of researchers, the importance of the RAE (Research Assessment Exercise) in UK universities, and the drive towards enhanced scholarly communication, all married with technological developments, result in fast moving developments in research information provision, storage, and access. This chapter gives a brief overview of some of the major factors that might have significant impacts on the scholarly research community and its modus operandi. Many developments are influenced by the political domain and drive (or lack of it) and the influence of economic factors plays a huge role in whether or not some new developments are able to gain ground and top level support.

JISC activities

A major strand of the JISC's work is the support and development of e-research. This is a rapidly developing field and over time researchers will see the fruits of JISC programmes and support resulting in new mainstream services. The JISC describes e-research as:

> the development of, and the support for, information and computing technologies to facilitate all phases of research processes. The term e-Research originates from the term e-Science but expands its remit to all research domains not just the sciences. It's concerned with technologies that support all the processes involved in research including (but not limited to) creating and sustaining research collaborations and discovering, analysing, processing, publishing, storing and sharing research data and information. Typical technologies in this domain include: Virtual Research Environments, Grid computing, visualisation services, and text and data mining services
>
> (JISC 2007b)

In addition to providing the network for UK HE and FE institutions, the JISC funds activities and programmes that 'support and innovate the use of ICT in education and research' (JISC 2007c) at a national level. JISC Collections[1] negotiates national deals with suppliers for licences and the purchase of digital collections. Such provision can enable institutions to provide e-resources to their users that would normally be beyond their budget. These collections are steadily growing.

Dissemination of research results

Researchers cannot of course find information if it is not made available in the first place. The dissemination of research results forms a major part of the research process. Academic freedom dictates that authors are free to publish their results wherever they wish. The motives for them choosing the channels they do are usually dictated by:

- Prestige of the publication (its impact factor, refusal rate, respect within the community, and peer review)
- Speed of publication enabling the authors to certify themselves as first to discover or publish on the topic

- Visibility of their research which enables other members of their research community to access their findings
- The requirement of a funding agency

Funding bodies' policies

In recent years there has been a marked change in policy regarding requirements relating to research materials produced as a result of funding by some agencies, and in June 2006 the Research Councils UK (RCUK) published a position statement on access to research results. This statement

> reaffirms the Research Councils' commitment to the guiding principles that publicly funded research must be made available and accessible for public examination as rapidly as practical; published research outputs should be effectively peer-reviewed; this must be a cost effective use of public funds; and outputs must be preserved and remain accessible for future generations
>
> (RCUK 2006)

Each council which makes up the RCUK has developed or is in the process of developing its own approach to this guiding principle. For example, the BBSRC (Biotechnology and Biological Sciences Research Council) requires that for outputs of research it funds 'a copy of any resulting published journal article or conference proceedings to be deposited, at the earliest opportunity, in an appropriate e-print repository, wherever such a repository is available' (BBSRC 2006). The MRC (Medical Research Council) takes a slightly different approach. It 'requires that electronic copies of any research papers accepted for publication in a peer-reviewed journal, which are supported in whole or in part by MRC funding, are deposited at the earliest opportunity – and certainly within six months – in UK PubMed Central (UKPMC)' (MRC 2006).

It is not only the RCUK which has changed its policy. In fact the first funder to adopt this new approach was the Wellcome Trust which currently:

- 'Expects authors of research papers to maximise the opportunities to make their results freely available and, where possible, to retain their copyright'
- 'Will provide grantholders with additional funding to cover open access charges levied by publishers who offer this option and can meet the Trust's requirements'
- 'Requires electronic copies of any research papers that have been accepted for publication in a peer-reviewed journal, and are supported in whole or in part by Wellcome Trust funding, to be made freely accessible from the PMC database (and any other PMC International (PMCI) sites, such as UKPMC) . . . as soon as possible, and in any event within six months of the journal publisher's official date of final publication'

(Wellcome Trust 2007b)

Funders such as these will pay 'author pays' fees if they are included in the application for funding.

Further afield, both the European Union and the NIH (National Institutes of Health) in the US are considering changes in policy for access to funded research. The EU published a communication on 'scientific information in the digital age: access, dissemination and preservation' (EU 2007a) and discussions continue. This document recommended a number of actions including provision of costs for publishing (including open access) and funding for infrastructure which includes open access repositories.

Discussion in the US is gathering pace, and at the time of writing two government reports have recently been published raising the issue of public access to publicly funded research. The NIH has since 2005 requested that authors provide free access to NIH funded research. If this policy is changed as supporters of open access wish it to be, the scholarly communication landscape in the US could be radically changed. There is even a group calling itself the Alliance for Taxpayer Access[2] which is calling for NIH funded research to be made available to the taxpayers which fund it.

The debate on scientific publishing is continuing and if major mandates are adopted may change author practice considerably. There is also the possibility that other disciplines may experience changes in requirements.

A website summarizing funders' archiving policies has been provided by SHERPA: it has been romantically named JULIET[3] (because it acts as a companion site to the well established SHERPA RoMEO site).

Access and dissemination policies have a marked influence on researchers, who are required to abide by their funders' conditions of grant. At the time of writing policies are still being developed by some of the councils and over time this particular landscape has the potential to change the dissemination of research drastically.

Open access

Open access is making materials, for example research findings and papers, freely available. It is a means of publishing and sharing research findings. The BOAI (Budapest Open Access Initiative) defines open access as

> free availability on the public internet, permitting any users to read, download, copy, distribute, print, search, or link to the full texts of these articles, crawl them for indexing, pass them as data to software, or use them for any other lawful purpose, without financial, legal, or technical barriers other than those inseparable from gaining access to the internet itself. The only constraint on reproduction and distribution, and the only role for copyright in this domain, should be to give authors control over the integrity of their work and the right to be properly acknowledged and cited
>
> (BOAI 2007)

There is a distinction between open access journals and open access repositories that hold self-archived and other items. Open access journals are similar to historically standard journals in that they can include peer review and offer the certification required by researchers. The differences are in:

1 The funding model: the costs of publication are met either by the author's institution or by the body which funded the research (although both methods can confusingly be called 'author pays')
2 Access which is free to all with no subscription or other payment necessary, nor any barrier such as a password required to access the content

Open access repositories are complementary to open access journals and can provide access to all types of scholarly materials such as articles (both post- and pre-prints), grey literature such as conference papers, book chapters, theses, datasets, and other items. Many institutions are providing their own repositories and are using them for a variety of purposes which include the dissemination, management, and preservation of the content.

Many publishers are providing some form of open access model which authors may select for their articles. There has been much heated discussion between the publishing community, proponents of open access, and other interested parties, and author decisions are being strongly influenced by the position of funding bodies (see above). It will take time for the situation to settle. As tensions between publishers, libraries, and authors are resolved over time, and government and other influential bodies become more involved, the mode of dissemination of research output could change markedly.

Many libraries are developing and promoting open access repositories for the purposes of:

- Increased visibility that results in increased impact and citations to items
- Retaining research materials (such as articles and other items) from one author, group or institution in a single location, as opposed to being spread across many separate and unlinked locations
- 'Branding' the items as emanating from the institution and providing a showcase for the research of that institution
- Enabling the research to be more easily discovered and accessed
- Providing a faster means of making research results available and thereby certifying the research on the part of the researcher
- Complying with funding bodies' requirements to make the results of publicly funded research available to the general public
- As a means of digital preservation

There are a myriad additional reasons. Setting up a basic repository has been technically relatively easy and many institutions now provide one. Filling them has been more of a problem partly because of the already significant pressures on academic authors, partly because management of the repositories has been shoe-horned into the jobs of individuals who are juggling many other fast moving digital development responsibilities but also because, at the time of writing, a critical mass has not yet been reached.

As more importance is placed on these repositories by institutions and advanced functionalities are incorporated which are attractive to users (for example, automatic updating of publication lists on personal Web pages), the repositories should be filled and become a vital part of the scholarly communication landscape which is complementary to traditional publishing.

The SPARC Initiative

SPARC (the Scholarly Publishing and Academic Resources Coalition)[4] aims to address some of the problems associated with current modes of disseminating scholarly information by encouraging change and new alternatives in scholarly communications. The coalition comprises universities, research libraries, and other organizations and has a partner in Europe: SPARC Europe.[5] SPARC Europe states that 'we advocate change in the scholarly communications market, support competition, and encourage new publishing models (in particular, open access models) that better serve the international researcher community' (SPARC Europe 2007).

Searching for research materials

Cross-searching

Cross-searching (sometimes known as federated or meta searching) is searching across a number of resources (such as databases) in a single action using a specially developed interface. This is convenient for the searcher, but technically causes some difficulties. The searcher benefits from saving time and effort by not having to search a multiplicity of databases with an equal number of interfaces. One of the problems is that the search is reduced to the lowest common denominator of search functionality of the databases included. Cross-searching is also a means of the user discovering resource providers of which they may have been previously unaware. Libraries are beginning to provide such facilities so that users may search other databases from the same interfaces as their catalogues. An additional issue is that of the user discovering the most appropriate source of information. Cross-searching has its uses and can be hugely valuable, but serious researchers may prefer to use the native interface of multiple individual databases.

Semantic Web and Web 2.0

The semantic Web (and subsequently, the semantic Grid) is a method of giving meaning to data accessible on the Web. Work is taking place on the development of ontologies, or the creation of shared, common vocabularies. The reason for this is (partly) to enable more effective discovery of information on the Web. It works by computers becoming 'much better able to process and "understand" the data that they merely display at present' (Berners-Lee et al. 2001: 2). If computers accurately ascertain and manipulate the semantics of the description of content, then information retrieval should result in more relevant information than the current process.

Web 2.0 is the term commonly used to describe a range of dynamic Web services and architecture which enable more intelligent and useful inter-operation and functionality between them. However, the term is not officially defined and can mean different things to different people. It might include image services, blogs, RSS feeds, geospatial products, and other services. Options such as theses are being considered and developed by research information providers and others to enhance services and make them increasingly seamless and useful to the researcher.

Text mining

The problem of the information explosion is making it increasingly difficult to process and extract relevant meaning and information from all relevant sources. Text mining is being developed to provide a solution for extracting information from large quantities of documents or other sources. The National Centre for Text Mining (NaCTeM) describes text mining as a method which 'attempt to discover new, previously unknown information by applying techniques from information retrieval, natural language processing and data mining' (NaCTeM 2007). These developments are of interest to the research community for aiding the retrieval of relevant information from an ever-growing corpus of literature and data.

Open URLs

The development of the Open URL framework allows a Web-based scholarly service to link to the most appropriate copy of a resource. A particular resource might be available via a number of sources, but the user might be permitted to access the resource by only one route (for example, via their own library). Use of an Open URL will enable the user to use that appropriate route automatically without them even having to consider the other unsuccessful routes that would lead them to a dead end. The benefits for researchers are many and the use of Open URLs will contribute to seamless linking and improved resource discovery in the information environment. All of this, however, should remain invisible to the user.

e-Books and e-theses

e-Books

e-Books have had a mixed inception and reception. There have been a variety of methods of delivery and viewing, and payment and protection models: Web-based systems are generally gaining popularity over handheld devices. There are benefits of using a digital book such as the search capabilities, the concept of micro purchase (that is, the purchase of a small section of a publication, say, a page at a time) and the possibility of linking to other multimedia sources.

Reference books have been the most favoured types of book to be made available electronically for the UK market and are a successful and popular product. Academic libraries are generally keen that more textbooks aimed at the UK market are made available to ease difficulties of mass provision. Publishers, however, are concerned about the possible impact on sales.

The discussion about what exactly constitutes an e-book is likely to develop further as providers produce more inventive products while maintaining the traditional online version of the print copy for some titles. The electronic format is here to stay, but how it is manifested will take promotion, negotiation, and time. More e-book collections are becoming available and in the UK the JISC is adding steadily to its collections and working on ways of promoting the use of e-books within academic institutions. Two areas are of particular note: the work towards increasing provision of electronic textbooks and mass digitization of out of copyright texts, together with added services. However, the future of the printed book seems assured, certainly for the foreseeable future.

e-Theses and dissertations

The new UK national thesis service, EThOS, will provide a means to store, access, and preserve digital theses produced at institutions in the UK. As well as digital delivery of theses, it has alternative methods of delivery including print and CD. It provides a digitization service for those items not available electronically and universities are subscribing to the service to ensure that their theses are made available in this way. The mode of operation works by enabling the awarding institution to submit digital theses (together with their record) to EThOS, thereby building a comprehensive collection. The digitization process is being 'kick-started' by additional funding provided by the JISC to pay for the digitization of over 5000 of the most popular (i.e., the most requested and print or microfilm format) items. EThOS will provide theses on an open access basis. It will work in tandem with institutions which may have their own repository of theses, but if not, may choose to use EThOS as the repository for their digital collection. The service is expected to move to full production service over the next few years. This general move towards electronic provision (and possibly submission) of theses will have an impact on the training required for postgraduate research students and their supervisors who will need to be aware of the issues associated with digital items such as formats, architecture of the thesis, and, most importantly, rights.

The importance of data

In recent years increasing amounts of data have been collected for the purposes of research. Dataset can for example comprise original raw data or perhaps a final anonymized and processed set: it could be a database or a collection of images or other format types. There is concern as to what happens to those data after the initial work has been completed. Sometimes it is submitted to a national data archive such as the UKDA (UK Data Archive). Sadly, much data is lost. This can be a real problem as future researchers may wish to do continuing work on the same data, the original data can be used to support or refute scholarly findings, or it can even result in the same work being performed twice. Because this situation has been identified and flagged up as of great importance there is much work underway to collect, store, curate, and preserve datasets produced as a result of research. This is no easy task and major bodies such as the Digital Curation Centre (DCC)[6] and Research Information Network (RIN)[7] are supporting work in this area. It is hoped that in the future more data will be collected and submitted by the researchers themselves, possibly even automatically as laboratory experiments are carried out, so that this large corpus of research material is not lost forever. Work is progressing on the eBank UK project which is exploring the links between research data and digital libraries.

The e-science programme and the Grid

Researchers have always drawn on the work of others. The development of the e-science programme and the Grid provides a means for collaboration and use of data for research on a global scale. It provides access to the experimental facilities and computing capability that enable this collaboration. The National e-Science Centre[8] states that 'in the future e-science will refer to the large scale science that will increasingly be carried out through distributed global collaborations enabled by the Internet. Typically, a feature of such collaborative scientific enterprises is that they will require access to very large data collections, very large scale computing resources and high performance visualisation back to the individual user scientists' (National e-Science Centre 2007). The facilities include storage for vast amounts of data and the means to run highly complex experiments using distributed computing facilities.

Also, application of Grid technology and the experiences of the e-science community are being applied within social science. The ESRC funds the National Centre for e-Social Science[9] which is running parallel work on how powerful Grid computing can be applied and developed for the social sciences.

'Grid computing is applying the resources of many computers in a network to a single problem at the same time' (Berman et al. 2003) and is the underlying technical architecture that supports the e-science programme. As well as sharing computing power, it will enable users to share databases and other tools. Use of the Grid is increasing as institutions set up centres to support and encourage researchers and as their needs become ever greater.

Collaborative e-research

The Grid will be one means of supporting collaborative e-research. As data gathering increases to almost unimaginable levels and more research is developed in new areas such as interdisciplinary subjects (for example, bioinformatics), the resulting 'data deluge' will need to be managed and maintained (Hey and Trefethen 2003). The benefits of scale of a number of centres working collaboratively will contribute to the success of such developments.

Means of managing and presenting information

Increasingly institutions are employing the use of systems such as VLEs (virtual learning environments), managed learning environments (MLEs), and portals or gateways as teaching and learning vehicles and for managing and presenting information. The researcher may encounter one or more of these systems (although not strictly designed specifically for the research community) which usually require some form of authentication such as a password. Usage and terminology varies widely and terms are often used interchangeably.

Another area which is becoming increasingly developed is that of virtual research environments (VREs). VREs are designed to help researchers manage their research including the information they use and the tasks they perform. It is technically something of a challenge to create a VRE which includes the services, functions, and tools required by researchers. A number of projects have been set up to investigate solutions and best practice: this is an area which could see much change over the coming years.

Digital preservation and curation

A major concern of those working in information is that of long-term preservation and curation of digital materials. Either the storage of information has to change to match the access facilities, or the method of storage has to be able to be accessed by whatever means available, perhaps by creating a way of emulating the original hardware or software, however long a period has elapsed since the materials were archived (Granger 2000). The three main threats to digital information are:

- Technical obsolescence
- The fragility of the data
- Lack of knowledge and good practice on the part of those who are responsible for it (DCC 2007a)

An example of the problem of technical obsolescence is the BBC's Domesday project. This took place in 1986 and the data was stored on the now superseded LV-ROM videodisc (Abbott 2003). Researchers finally solved this particular problem with work carried out at the Universities of Leeds (UK) and Michigan (US).

There is much activity in the field of digital preservation. In the UK a body has been set up called the Digital Preservation Coalition (DPC) 'to foster joint action to address the urgent challenges of securing the preservation of digital resources in the UK and to work with others internationally to secure our global digital memory and knowledge base' (DPC 2002). Members of the DPC include institutions such as the British Library, the National Archives, the JISC, and the Publishers Licensing Society (PLS).

One other member of the DPC is the Digital Curation Centre (DCC) whose purpose 'is to provide a national focus for research and development into curation issues and to promote expertise and good practice, both national and international, for the management of all research outputs in digital format' (DCC 2007b). The DCC provides services to help those who hold digital data to manage and preserve that data successfully resulting in it being both available and usable long-term.

Research Information Network (RIN)

The Research Information Network was set up in 2005: its remit is to find methods of dealing with the increasing amount and complexity of research information. The group's stated aim is 'to lead and co-ordinate new developments in the collaborative provision of research information for the benefit of researchers in the UK' (RIN 2007). Such a national body has the potential to lead a coordinated approach for improved research information provision in the UK. The RIN has initially been set up for a three year period.

Journal impact factors, peer review, and citation services

Academics have been familiar with journal impact factors for some time. This is a means of scoring journals using ratings and is used by authors to aid selection of journals for publication. This model of measurement is being challenged as more research becomes freely available and with the potential of using Web access and download logs to either complement or replace all or part of other measurements. The RAE may undergo fundamental changes in design for the next round in order to incorporate bibliographic measurements: much work is needed in this area. Arguments rage as to whether it is best to leave to the status quo or to take advantage of the online domain.

All parties concerned agree that peer review is vital to ensure quality and accuracy of scholarship within the publication process. However, the traditional process of peer review is under scrutiny as open access gains strength. Again the potential of the online domain is being considered as a possible means of updating current practice. One example of a new model of peer review is that used by BioMedCentral publications in the BMC series which use open peer review where, instead of anonymous reviewing, reviewers sign their reviews and the history of the item prior to publication (including previous versions, and reviewers and authors comments) is available for access. Open peer review has been common practice in some circles for many years: it will take time for the dust to settle and see whether a new model achieves popularity and credibility.

There are a number of issues associated with the current practice of provision of citation services. Work is beginning to create more reliable and wider information on citations using the digital domain, although this is a complex problem which will need creative solutions that are satisfactory to the many interested parties. The potential for valuable and integrated services is great. For an example of some of the work currently underway see the OpCit Project.[10]

Summary checklist

Chapter	
1	Is your title/question clear and unambiguous? Are you clear what the research is about?
	What is the purpose of the research? Who is the final product aimed at? Use the questions within Chapter 1 to help define the purpose.
	What is the scope and extent of the research? Use the questions within Chapter 1 to help define the scope.
	Have you dealt with all practicalities such as finding out usernames and passwords for electronic resources?
2	Do you know where in your library to find printed resources for your research?
	What relevant online resources are available to you at your home library?
	Do you know how to access the online resources you need? Do you need a special password?
	Are there specialist collections at other libraries that you should investigate?
	Have you identified and met any library staff who will be able to help you with your research?
	Is any training in using library resources available?
	Are you familiar with:
	• The classification system?
	• The catalogue and how to use it efficiently and effectively? Are you aware of the limits of a library catalogue?
	• Any specialist library services you may require?
3	Have you checked indexes and databases of current research?
	Have you found out about current research funded by funding agencies and other bodies?
	Have you identified relevant theses?
4	What will the end product be: a brief resumé, a document of a few thousand words or a large scale work such as a thesis, in depth report or a book? How much research/time/information is appropriate for this type of work?
	How much time is available for the project?
	What types of materials will be required?
	Will you need access to any difficult to obtain primary sources?

Chapter

Are there sources of information in other disciplines that are relevant?

Have you set clear limits been for the research? What are you *not* going to include? Where are the boundaries of the research?

Have you made a record of what is already known and relevant to this project?

Do you have a general idea of your information finding strategy?

5   Which databases, abstracts, and indexes are most relevant to your research? Are there other more general databases which will also be useful?

Is there a federated search option at your institutional library (where you can search across a number of databases at one go)?

Select a key database for your research and find out about the fields it indexes, whether or not it has a thesaurus, if there is useful information on the help function, and how you can manage the records you retrieve (marking, emailing, using bibliographic software). Are there any quirks that you should know about?

Do you know how to find open access journals and other open access materials?

Which national library catalogues and collections and specialist research collections should you check?

Which sources of information about other types of materials will you use (e.g., archives, official documents, grey literature, images, or maps).

6   Having read around the subject, you should now have a record of significant words which may be used for searching.

Identify the concepts and keywords and work through the steps in Figure 6.2.

Incorporate Boolean and other connectors as well as devices such as truncation and wildcards to focus the search and retrieve relevant records.

Set limits on the search or use the NOT connector to ignore extraneous records.

Do you need to refine, broaden, or narrow your searches? Are the results what you expected?

Evaluate the results at each stage using what is found to modify and improve the search strategy.

Have you saved all the relevant records so that you have all the information necessary for acquiring the full text?

Have you got to the point where you are not retrieving new records?

Are there any other databases or other sources you should use?

7   Check the references in the work(s) you are using and identify any which you want to investigate further.

Where might you check to see if the article(s) has/have been cited anywhere else?* Can you find any actual citations of this/these article(s)?

Could any of the articles be defined as an original key work? If not, can you identify an original key work in the topic?

Chapter

Using the references you discovered at* above, are there any other works cited in those works which might be of interest?

8   Have you checked all possible catalogues and online sources at your home institution including online full text e-journal and e-book collections?

Are any of the materials you require available open access either in an open access journal or via an open access repository?

Are you aware of any relevant specialist collections or archives?

9   Have you considered using more than one search engine?

Have you recorded detailed references of where you found the information on the WWW?

Have you been critical enough of what you have retrieved on the WWW?

10   Have you checked what is easily available at your home institution?

Can you access items that you require freely on the Internet using a reputable open access repository?

What other resources will you need to use to access the information you require?

Will you need to order any items using interlibrary loan or other document supply service?

Have you checked what is easily available at your home institution?

Can you access items that you require freely on the Internet using a reputable open access repository?

What other resources will you need to use to access the information you require?

Will you need to order any items using interlibrary loan or other document supply service?

11   Are you satisfied that the information you have gathered or intend to gather satisfies your criteria in provenance, content, and relation to the subject?

Can you access and do you have permission to use the information you have found?

12   What style of referencing are you using? Why?

Have you referenced every work you have cited?

Will you include a list of works of further interest to your readers which you haven't actually cited?

Do you have the full details of all the references you cite?

Is your referencing consistent? Have you consistently used the correct typeface and punctuation?

Have you identified a source of help for referencing queries (librarian, academic, reference work, etc.)?

Are you using bibliographic software (see Chapter 13)?

Chapter

13   How will you save a record of your searches?

Do you have the *full* details of all sources used?

If you have any photocopied extracts of works you are intending to cite, do you have details of the work from which they were taken?

If you are using references taken from a chapter have you recorded the details of the book in which the chapter is included?

Do you wish to make use of bibliographic software?

14   Are you sure you have obtained permissions to use materials in which copyright is held by another party?

Have you acknowledged the copyright holder where relevant?

Will you want to use one of the Creative Commons or other licences for your work? If so, which one?

Have you read any copyright transfer agreement carefully and do you know what rights you have to use your work after submission to the publisher?

Do you wish to retain the copyright of your own work or grant an exclusive or non-exclusive licence to the publisher (if submitting to a publisher for publication)?

Are there any parts of your work for which you should apply for other IP protection (for example, patent or design)?

Can you be sure that you haven't plagiarized work by others?

15   Have you signed up for relevant alerts?

Are there any useful discussion lists in your subject area?

How will you find out about conferences and events which are relevant to you?

How best can you keep informed about current developments in your subject?

Appendix 1: Using a library

Library resources • Library services • The organization of resources in a library • Using a library catalogue

Library resources

A collection may comprise items in one, some, or all of the following categories:

- Hard copy (including print resources including books, journals, maps, manuscripts)
- Electronic (including databases, CD-ROMs, DVD, and other formats)
- **Microform** (microfilm, microfiche, and microprint)
- Multimedia (including video, audio cassette, vinyl disc, film, photographs)
- Artefacts (including teaching resources, geological specimens, toys)

The researcher may or may not know the type of resource they require, but they will need to become familiar in how to use the formats in which the information they need is stored. Sometimes there is a choice of format and the most appropriate should be selected. For example, if there were a choice between a CD-ROM or Internet/Web-based version, the Internet version might be more current. Likewise, the hard copy of a newspaper may be preferable if the online version does not include all the diagrams that accompany the article.

Library services

The issue desk

The issue desk is often the main frontline service of the library. This is where users borrow and return items and carry out other transactions such as placing reservations or collecting reserved items. Many libraries provide a self-service issue and returns facility to supplement the staffed issue desk.

Researchers should be aware of their **loan entitlement** (such as numbers of items and length of loan) and any restrictions that apply so that they can make full use of the library and its resources. Being aware of borrowing rights and observing due dates can save time and expense by avoiding withdrawal of privileges and unnecessary fines.

Interlibrary loans (ILL) and document supply

If access to an item is not provided either physically or electronically by the home library, a solution can be a document delivery service. For many libraries this is made possible using their **interlibrary loan** service. The researcher should be familiar with the procedures for ILL and document supply at their home library. This should include their allowance (these services are charged to libraries and so there is usually a set quota per person or fee per item) and the ability to obtain extra items for payment. Time allowances should be made for obtaining items not held by the home library (see Chapter 10).

Services for those with special needs

Libraries can be inhospitable places for those with physical or learning difficulties. Users may encounter difficulties with the buildings or with access to and use of the resources. Libraries are developing ways in which they can solve, or at least, ease such problems.

Intermediaries who liaise with the library

Depending on the institution, there may be a body such as a student advice service that assesses the needs of the individual and negotiates additional services or use of specialist technology for that person.

Specialist technology and adaptation of websites

Increasingly sophisticated technology is being developed for use by those who have special needs and libraries are increasing their provision of such equipment. The technology may include:

- Specialist hardware such as Braille machines, large visual display units, adapted keyboards
- Provision of standard hardware that eases the situation for those with difficulties. For example, scanners or colour printers
- Specialist software such as mapping/planning programmes or screen readers
- Adaptation of Web pages, for example, a text only version and facilities such as user selection of background colours

Additional library services

Some libraries run additional services for those who require them. These may include such services as a fetch and collect service to save the user from having to navigate through a large building, negotiate shelving stacks, and/or use a complex **classification system**.

The organization of resources in a library

The resources stored in a library may be sorted by subject or by some other criteria. Whatever the method, the library's **catalogue** is the key to finding what is available (including electronic resources) and the **shelfmark** (or **call number**) which is assigned to each physical item to locate it, either by the user or by requesting the item via a member of library staff. The aim of such schemes is to aid efficient retrieval of items.

Open or closed access

Libraries vary in the amount of access they allow their users. Some are open access and have all their stock on display for users to handle and browse. These libraries are inclined to use a classification system that groups stock according to subject content. **Closed access** libraries require that users request items and wait while a member of staff fetches them. Many are a combination of the two. If a user requires closed access items they should leave ample time for ordering and collection. Depending on the location of the closed access items, there may only be a few collections per day during office hours.

Browse or search

A closed access collection demands that the user search the catalogue for relevant items. Open access gives some choice. If the choice is available, the user should scour the catalogue for all the relevant items they can discover. Having found the appropriate shelfmarks, it can be beneficial to peruse the shelves in those areas as there is always the possibility that relevant titles on a similar topic have been overlooked when searching. This is particularly true of items that use unexpected words in their titles or records or for catalogues that have a limited subject searching facility.

The classification system

In a library classification is the means of grouping items by subject area. It is the task of the classifier to assign a classification number to each item so that it can be shelved in an orderly fashion according to subject and, just as importantly, easily retrieved by users.

Serials may be shelved separately, perhaps without using a classification system. For example, they may be shelved in alphabetical order of title.

The subject nature of classification

Use of a classification system such as Dewey Decimal Classification (see below) should, in theory, result in items in a similar subject area being shelved in close proximity.

However, in practice browsing should not be relied on. As classification is more an art than a science, the location of an item is dependent on the classifier. For example a book on the psychological impact of medical treatment could either be shelved with others on psychology or with those on medicine. Also, when a classification system is updated, as they are from time to time, the result may be that items are shelved at more than one number and the library has to consider whether or not to re-number large amounts of stock. To counter these problems the library's catalogue should always be used to check the correct locations.

Methods of classification

There are a number of systems in use in libraries and users may need to become familiar with one or more of them. They vary from the well known Dewey Decimal Classification (DDC) and Library of Congress (LC) systems to inhouse schemes not used in any other library. Both DDC and LC are constructed using a hierarchical arrangement working from the general to the more specific.

Dewey Decimal Classification

In this system knowledge is divided up using a system based on ten main classes. As more detail of the subject matter is included, the numbers have figures added to them resulting in a number of up to three digits followed by a decimal point and any number of digits. For example, the DDC edition 21 places the medical condition leukaemia at 362.19699419 (medical services emphasis) or 616.99419 (medicine and health emphasis).

The main classes are:

0 Computer science, information, and general works
1 Philosophy and psychology
2 Religion
3 Social sciences
4 Language
5 Science

6 Technology
7 Arts and recreation
8 Literature
9 History and geography

These numbers do not operate in the same way as mathematical numbers. For example, the number 42 (four two and not forty-two) will be found further along the sequence from 401 (four zero one, not four hundred and one). When searching for an item, each digit should be taken in turn.

LC classification

The LC classification scheme is based on the division of subjects into areas using 21 letters of the alphabet:

A   General works
B   Philosophy, psychology, religion
C   Auxiliary sciences of history
D   History (general) and history of Europe
E   History of America (US)
F   History of America (including British, French and Dutch America, and Latin America)
G   Geography, anthropology, recreation
H   Social sciences
J   Political science
K   Law
L   Education
M   Music and books on music
N   Fine arts
P   Language and literature
Q   Science
R   Medicine
S   Agriculture
T   Technology
U   Military science
V   Naval science
Z   Bibliography, library science, information resources (general)

Each class is broken down into sub-classes such as fine art:

• NA for architecture
• NB for sculpture

At this point, numbers are added for each narrower subject, for example:

- NA 1995 Architecture as a profession
- NA 7100–7884 Domestic architecture. Houses. Dwellings

Variations of classification

Some libraries adapt classification systems to suit their own purposes while others have created their own systems. There are systems which have been developed to serve specific subject areas for example the *British Catalogue of Music Classification* by E.J. Coates or the Moys system of classification for use in law libraries developed by Elizabeth Moys.

The shelfmark of an item may also include a suffix as well as the **classification number**. This may be the first three letters of the author's name or the title and imposes further order, particularly when there are many items at one class number.

Classification numbers may be long, complex, and unmemorable, so always have a pencil and paper handy to jot down the numbers of the items required.

Use of separate sequences

A classification system allows the library to shelve all its stock in order starting at the beginning of the sequence until it reaches the end. In practice, this is rarely what happens. Library collections often comprise a number of shorter sequences. These may be a main sequence plus collections of:

- short loan or reference use only items
- audio visual materials
- oversized or folio books shelved together in order to save space
- official publications
- statistics
- special or rare collections
- newspapers

and so on.

The library's catalogue should contain information regarding the physical location, including the sequence in which the item has been shelved. Check carefully, as much time and energy can be wasted looking for an item in the incorrect place.

Special collections

Many libraries have collections that have been acquired over the years and retain some unique feature. It may be, for example, a bequest of a collector of early editions, a collection of books in a particular subject area, ancient and valuable manuscripts, or the works of a particular scholar or author. These special collections are often shelved discretely not within the main collection.

They may be closed access when other parts of the library are not. They may also require some additional arrangements for access such as a letter from a home library or used only in a specified area of the building. Find out about any special arrangements before visiting a library and requesting access to any special collections.

Numbers in use around the library

Apart from shelfmarks, there are many other numbering systems in use in a library.

Item number

Classification or call numbers should not be confused with an item number. Libraries usually assign a unique identification number to each individual item. This is a means of identifying one particular copy of a **work**. For example, a library may hold eight copies of the fourth edition of Donald J. Shoemaker's book, *Theories of Delinquency: An Examination of Explanations of Delinquent Behavior*. All the copies will probably have the same classification number. However, they will each have a unique identification number, most often a barcode number.

ISBN and ISSN

Most catalogues will include details of a monograph's ISBN (International Standard Book Number) and a serial's ISSN (International Standard Serial Number), a unique number assigned to each title.

1 ISBN

- Varies within the same title with each format (i.e., hardback, paperback) and each edition (first and subsequent editions, international student edition, etc.)
- A string of ten digits (the last digit is sometimes replaced by a letter 'X') for example, 0 099 75181 X
- In January 2007 a new system was implemented which increased the ISBN to 13 digits, for example, 978 0-335-21684-0
- e-ISBNs are often assigned to electronic books

2 ISSN

- Unique for each title
- All issues of a serial publication will have the same ISSN
- Comprises two sets of four-digit numbers separated by a hyphen, for example, *Advances in Physics* ISSN 0001–8732
- The last digit may be a letter 'X'
- e-ISSNs are often assigned to electronic journals

If an item does not have an ISBN or ISSN the library will assign a control number of its own to identify the title.

Using a library catalogue

A library catalogue is a list of items which that library stocks, whatever format. Each work has a catalogue record comprising bibliographic (or other) details of the work. Most medium and large libraries have progressed from a card index, via microfiche or other format to an online public access catalogue, commonly known as an OPAC. The catalogue is the user's key to the library – it provides the mechanism to discover what the library stocks and the status and location of each item. Researchers should ensure they are competent and efficient users of library catalogues, whatever system is used.

Some historic and smaller private collections may have a printed list rather than an OPAC or other electronic database. If the catalogue of an information provider is only available in print, either a copy will have to be obtained or a visit made to the collection in order to view the catalogue.

The OPAC

Web OPACs can be accessed from anywhere with Internet access. It is customary to allow open access to such OPACs, that is, without the need for a password. Although this does not guarantee a user's right to access the materials held in the library, it is a vital discovery tool.

OPACs, although invaluable, are not able to perform the refined searches of the bibliographic databases (see Chapter 6). This means that there are limits to their ability to provide information and it is important to be aware of these restrictions. The information stored on the OPAC is dependent on the quality of the **catalogue record**.

The information contained on the OPAC

The following information may be found using an OPAC:

- A bibliographic (or otherwise) description of the item
- Numbers of copies
- Location of items
- Status of items (for example, on loan to another user, on order, or not yet in stock)
- Details of serial holdings
- Personal borrower record

- Reading list information, that is, details of the reading list on which an item appears, the name of the lecturer plus access to that lecturer's complete lists

The OPACs of specialist libraries may also include information such as:

- Binding information
- Details of provenance and ownership for items of historical interest
- Details of others associated with the item, such as printers and booksellers

Linking to full text of e-resources

Online catalogues are useful for linking to electronic formats. A member of a library can often navigate easily from the catalogue to the full text of electronic works. Users will only be able to access these resources:

- If they are entitled to
- If they have the appropriate username and password where required
- If the computer they are using to access the catalogue is not 'tied down' to catalogue use only

The holdings of a print and electronic version of a publication may vary. Users should check the electronic holdings as they would the print version.

What is a catalogue record?

A catalogue record is a description of a work. There are standard details that should appear in a properly constructed record that allow the user to identify and locate a particular work using a number of entry points (such as the author).

The information a catalogue record contains

A catalogue record for a book may include details of:

- The author
- The title of the work
- The edition number
- Details of publication
- Physical description (size, number of pages, and so on)
- Series information
- Notes (for example, 'previous edition 1989')
- Shelfmark and ISBN

The record may be constructed to ease discovery by the user. Therefore it may include information such as additional authors or an alternative spelling of the author's name. Libraries use author authority files so that works by different authors with the same name are not confused. It may contain subject headings assigned to the item (see below).

Subject access

The subject headings included in a catalogue record may come from an approved list which ensures consistency (both within one library and between different libraries), for example, the Library of Congress Subject Headings (LCSH) which are becoming an international standard and are included in British Library catalogue records. Another widely adopted system of subject headings is the MeSH (Medical Subject Headings) thesaurus developed by the National Medical Library in the US. Users can take advantage of the controlled vocabulary to search for items in the subject they require. Specialist libraries may include additional information such as terms from the Rare Books and Manuscripts Section (RBMS) of the ACRL (Association of College and Research Libraries).

Universal bibliographic records

Although an ideal world is one where every publication, be it a book, leaflet, or website, has a perfect bibliographic description attached to it, this is not the reality. Most **ephemeral** publications and **grey literature** do not have any record associated with them at the point of publication. For this reason it can be difficult to locate these items.

Searching the library catalogue

Good catalogue records provide the user with a number of entry points depending on the information they have available. The user may know the full details of the item they wish to access, they may want to find out what the library stocks in a particular subject area or may want to find a number of books by the same author. Be aware of the different search options so that the most appropriate can be selected, resulting in efficient and effective searching of the catalogue. As with all searching, check the help available to find the most effective means of searching. There may be advice on phrase searching, on the use of **stopwords**, default settings, and other help (see Chapter 6).

Selecting the appropriate catalogue

Although many large libraries have a single catalogue where all their stock is listed, small and specialist libraries may offer a number of different catalogues. For example, the London Library[1] currently has three catalogues:

- The Online Computer Catalogue – for the majority of material acquired since 1950
- The Printed and Card Catalogues – for material acquired before 1950 and items not yet on the online catalogue acquired between 1950–83

Anyone using this library would have to note that the catalogues are defined by the date the material was acquired by the library, not when it was published. This library has been running a major project to transfer all its records to the online catalogue.

In addition to the main catalogue, libraries may have sub-catalogues which allow the user to limit their search to, for example, journals or audio visual materials. This is a valuable tool for reducing the numbers of irrelevant results. The British Library[2] allows options to search for items that are reference use only or that are available via document supply services.

Catalogues may or may not include details of other resources, for example:

- Electronic resources: may be on a separate list or Web page
- Artefacts may not be included

Searching by author

An author search option usually allows the use of an editor's name. An unusual family name (or surname) can be searched for on its own resulting in a manageable number of results. Searching using a common name is less successful. The search can be narrowed down using the author's initials or first name, but be aware that the catalogue record will contain the author's name as it appears in the item. For a single author, this may vary from record to record, for example:

- Lawrence, D. H.
- Lawrence, David Herbert
- Lawrence, David
- Lawrence, D.
- Lawrence, David H.

This example run using the British Library Integrated Catalogue produces the results shown in Table A1.1.

There is always the possibility that there is some error in the spelling of the author's name resulting from:

- Incorrect details given to the searcher
- A name that has a homonym, e.g., Pierce/Pearce
- A foreign name that may be spelt in different ways in English transliteration such as Tchaikovsky/Tchaikowsky/Chaikovsky
- A typographical error on the part of the searcher

Table A1.1 Example of a search using an author's name

Search term (author field)	Numbers of hits
Lawrence	21,132
Lawrence, D. H.	1,018
Lawrence, David	122
Lawrence, David Herbert	1,467
Lawrence, D.	1,271
Lawrence, David H.	1,552

Source: British Library Integrated Catalogue Author search, exact phrase, 06.04.07

- A double-barrelled or other hyphenated name (e.g., Al-Amin)
- An error on the part of the cataloguer

A Web-based catalogue may include the author name as a link. Clicking on the link will retrieve other records of works by the same author.

Searching by keyword

This method of searching looks for words anywhere in the record or only in the title, depending on the catalogue. Between one and four words should be selected to act as keywords. The more uncommon the word(s), the fewer results will be retrieved. Keyword searching may be used to search for a particular item or as a form of subject search. If the keyword search looks for words only in the title, items on a similar topic that do not have the chosen word(s) in the title will not be retrieved. If the default setting of the search facility is 'AND' the addition of more keywords will narrow the search (see Chapter 6). If a term is included in the title of an item, the item is likely to be relevant.

Some catalogues automatically incorporate plurals and alternative spellings in the search: check before searching.

Searching by author/keyword

When the user knows the publication they wish to retrieve, the author/keyword option can be a reliable method of retrieval. This combination of two fields is useful for listing items by a single author on a particular topic, allowing the discovery of other works by the same author in the same area, although the caveats for keyword and author searching given above still apply.

Searching by title

A title search allows the users to be specific regarding the item they wish to retrieve, but the drawback can be that, unless the search **query** is identical to the title in the catalogue record, the item will not be retrieved. Searching using the first three or four words from the title will often suffice. Some catalogues have the title/keyword search field combined. The British Library Public Catalogue and the COPAC[3] (CURL – Consortium of University Research Libraries – OPAC) union catalogue title search fields accept keywords from the title.

Subject searching

A comprehensive subject search depends on records including reliable subject information. There may be differences in the subject headings used. For example, one item may use LCSH and another a different set of terms. This type of search is useful for retrieving records that are about a similar topic, but which do not necessarily include the chosen term as a word in the title.

A Web-based catalogue may include subject headings as links. Clicking on the link will retrieve other records with the same heading.

Classification searching

Classification searching is useful for retrieving the records of items shelved at the same classification number and therefore probably containing similar subject matter. It will not retrieve items on a similar subject classified at a different number.

IBSN/ISSN searching

This type of search will retrieve exact matches and records may not be linked. For example a search using the ISBN 0335193978 will retrieve a record for the paperback edition of Orna and Stevens' book, *Managing Information for Research* (Orna with Stevens 2000) if the library has a record for this edition of the book. It will only retrieve the record for the hardback version (ISBN 0335193986) if the numbers have been linked in some way. If the records are not linked, the library may hold a copy of the book the user requires, but does not retrieve details from the catalogue. The same is true of different editions of titles.

Limiting the search

Some catalogues allow for the setting of limits to a search so that the user can be more prescriptive. Limits may include:

- Selecting a specific location
- Searching a sub-catalogue (see above)
- Date of publication (a specified year or range of years)
- Details of the publisher
- Language

Spelling, abbreviations, punctuation

See Chapter 6.

Other information or services available on the catalogue

Library catalogues vary with the functions that they offer users. Some of the more common functions are explained below.

Further information about the title

The information that is displayed on the screen is not always the full details of the work held on the catalogue. There may be an option to reveal other details such as the full record.

Loan type

Many libraries use a number of different loan types, for example, ordinary (or long) loan, short loan, or desk loan (while some items will be reference use only). Check this information on the catalogue, as the different loan types may be shelved in various locations.

Numbers of copies

The user can determine the numbers of copies of a work held by the library and how many are available for loan.

Due date

If an item is out on loan, the date when the item is due for return is given. This can determine whether or not the user considers it worthwhile placing a reservation on the item (see below).

Reservations/held items

An OPAC will usually allow a user to place a reservation on an item and discover how many reservations are already placed by others. They may find out if another user has reserved an item that they themselves have on loan (the consequence of this may be that the user is not permitted to renew the item). The user may be able to request that the library holds the item for them to collect later, although not all libraries offer this service.

Status: on order/missing/withdrawn

Other status information may be:

- On order: the library has placed an order for the work and is awaiting its arrival
- Missing: the library previously held a copy of the item, but it has gone astray
- Withdrawn/deleted: the library previously held a copy of the item, but it has been withdrawn (this could be for a number of reasons, such as bad state of repair, copies removed to make additional space for new editions, and so on)

ILL requests

Some libraries run a system via their library management system that allow eligible users to request items via interlibrary loan. A signed copyright agreement will have to be supplied.

The personal borrower record

Members of a library may be able to access their personal borrower record via the OPAC. This allows them to check:

- The items they have out on loan
- The due dates of the items they have out on loan
- Whether another individual has placed a reservation on an item they have out on loan
- Renewal of loaned items

A personal username and password will probably be required to access the borrower record.

What the user will not find on the catalogue

Extensive though many catalogues are, there is some information not discernable using the catalogue. This includes:

- Details of who currently has an item out on loan. Libraries will not give out details of a user to other individuals
- Information such as the book being returned ten minutes ago and awaiting shelving
- The fact that someone has shelved the item in the incorrect place and it cannot be found at its correct shelfmark
- That the item is lying on a photocopier/desk having been used by someone else

And possibly:

- 'In' references, that is, details of individual chapters in a book

- Records of individual articles in journals
- Individual contents of music CDs/records (that is, the separate tracks)

although some libraries catalogue items to this detail.

Other types of catalogue

This Appendix has focused on OPACs but there are other forms of library catalogue in existence.

Card index

The user has to visit the library in order to access the catalogue. There will usually be at least two indexes: author index and title/subject index. The index should contain cross-references.

Printed catalogue

Users may be able to obtain (either free or for a fee) a copy of a printed index. This type of catalogue may become quickly out of date.

Microfiche

The user probably has to visit the library to access the catalogue. The currency depends on how frequently the microfiches are reprinted.

Bibliography

Some small libraries do not possess a library catalogue, but produce a bibliography with some details of the items held by the library.

Appendix 2: Formats of information sources

Introduction • Issues under consideration • Print/hard copy (text-based)
• Electronic (not including audio and visual materials) • Audio visual
formats • Artefacts • People

Introduction

The format of material is the storage medium in which information or data is retained. Even before the onset of electronic storage there was a plethora of formats for storing information. One could go back as far as clay tablets and papyrus, but this book concerns itself with the common formats encountered by researchers in the twenty-first century and issues associated with each. Many documents are available in multiple formats, for example, a journal such as the *Official Journal of the European Union L and C Series* is available in print, on the Internet, and on CD-ROM (EU 2007b).

The formats included in this appendix are:

- Print (text-based and including manuscripts and incunabula, microforms, maps, and atlases)
- Electronic (not including audio and visual materials)
- Audio visual formats (audio, image, moving image)
- Artefacts

Issues under consideration

Researchers will be familiar with the most common formats in which information and data are stored such as the print versions of books and journals. Those with specialist interests will be familiar with using formats such as music recordings, images, and maps. Depending on the subject area, be prepared to find information in many different formats, some of more recent development than others. Each is examined using some or all of the following criteria:

- currency
- ease of use
- accessibility
- ease of searching the content
- bibliographic records/description
- longevity
- price
- the role of the publisher

It becomes clear when using criteria such as those above, why some formats have existed as long as they have. And given this tested longevity, it can be explained why archivists are reluctant to adopt modern alternatives for long-term storage without their proven success.

Print/hard copy (text-based)

Monographs

A monograph is a publication that is complete in itself or forms part of a finite number of parts. Depending on the content, the publisher, and the dedication of the author(s), it may take around 18 months for a book to move from conception or proposal to the supplier's shelves. During this period, the content may have dated or have been superseded and authors have to be particularly careful when including information such as URLs (Universal Resource Locators) and screenshots of electronic sources which could easily prove redundant when the book is published.

There has been much talk of the death of the book. This is unlikely given people's unwillingness to read long documents onscreen, coupled with the convenient, portable nature of a book. Books will continue to be a viable format, although scholarly authors may prefer to take advantage of the features of an electronic format for certain publications (see e-books, Chapters 10 and 16). A book that is currently in print and for which the user has the bibliographic details should be relatively easy to obtain. Problems can arise with books that are no longer in print, particularly if they are antique or rare. On the other hand, book details are often released prior to publication and researchers may be left waiting with the promise of a book only to discover many months later that publication has been abandoned.

Foreign language titles may cause some difficulty: recourse to a specialist book supplier might prove successful. If the bibliographic details are sketchy, one can refer to the catalogue of a foreign national library or a publisher's website. The Internet has been a boon in this area as a search can be run which often results in useful details of the publication or holdings in some corner of the world.

Researchers should check for new editions of books that have been in print for a few years. Successful titles will often be revised or updated. If a previous edition is required, obtaining such titles can be difficult. Some titles go out of print surprisingly quickly when publishers commit to small print runs.

Print on demand may be a means of keeping titles, especially those with a small readership, permanently in print. It is a convenient method of allowing access to back lists or titles that would previously have been deemed out of print. At the present time it is not common, although online commercial booksellers are including print on demand titles in their current lists. This facility may increase in popularity providing customers are happy to download large documents or if publishers adopt the technology to produce books in this way. Another alternative that may develop is that of customers being given the option to purchase a section of a book via print on demand rather than the entire item.

The traditional search facility of a monograph is that of the index. A well constructed index enables the reader to locate topics of interest within the text. Obviously the index cannot list every word and phrase in the text (although see the section on e-books below) and its use requires some skill on the part of the reader to refer to suitable terms.

Monographs by established publishers usually have a bibliographic description provided by a national library. These descriptions allow for reliable cataloguing and therefore easy search and retrieval. Problems of a lack of bibliographic descriptions occur with grey literature and ephemera (works not published by the common commercial means) and can result in the item being difficult to discover and obtain.

Printed materials have a proven record of longevity providing they are properly stored and curated. Hardback publications are more robust than paperback or flimsy products, but all can last for long periods of time. Those wishing to access rare historical items will be expected to take the proper precautions such as the use of a suitable book rest or the wearing of gloves.

In general, the publisher takes the risk when publishing a work and will assess the market, as well as obtaining reviews of the content of a title prior to publication. Some titles are published by the author and such titles will not have been through the review process. Readers should therefore be aware of a work's pedigree.

Monographs may include: textbooks, novels, scholarly works, encyclopaedias, dictionaries, Festschrift (published in honour of a scholar), handbooks.

Serial publications

The term 'serial' as defined by Hawkins and Hirons from the Library of Congress refers to

> a continuing resource issued in a succession of discrete parts, usually bearing numbering, that has no predetermined conclusion. Examples of serials include journals, magazines, electronic journals, continuing directories, annual reports, newspapers, and monographic series
>
> (Hawkins and Hirons 2002)

A serial publication usually contains more recent material than that in monographs: it may be a matter of months between conception and publication. Even so, the researcher should be aware of this time lag. Daily newspapers, however, take only a single day (or even less) before publication.

Accessibility to printed serials is variable. While many of the major journals in a particular subject area may be stocked by a researcher's home library, access to more obscure, foreign language titles, and back runs may be more difficult. It is often the case in libraries that particular titles or even particular issues are more accessed than others and these items quickly become worn. Like any printed item, they are open to abuse and vandalism and many a researcher has despaired at the missing copy. Problems such as this can usually be rectified, but inconvenience the user.

Individual copies are given a number or date and may be gathered together to form volumes. Libraries send bundles of individual issues that form a whole volume for binding into a single hardback item. This is a disruptive process as the copies will be absent from the library for some time.

Many periodical publications provide a printed index to their contents, often at the end of the volume or calendar year. As with monographs, the usefulness of the index relies on the skills of both the indexer and the user. There may be a cumulative index that covers all volumes. Most online databases incorporate the details of print titles in their contents, and are a means of searching for bibliographic details. Most academic journals require an **abstract** of each article. Sometimes these abstracts are published separately.

Serial publications sometimes change their title. This can lead to confusion when accessing a title as the user may be unsure as to whether or not they are referring to the correct title. It is common to encounter abbreviations for serial titles. To ascertain the full title, use a publication such as *Periodical Title Abbreviations*, a three-volume work with entries listed by abbreviation and title (Alkire 2006) or an online source such as *Journal Abbreviation Sources* (McKiernan 2004).

The cost of subscription to academic journals is currently the subject of heated discussion between publishers, libraries, and academics. The price of subscription typically rises higher than the rate of inflation and this has an impact on library budgets. The cost of subscription to an individual is usually less than that of an institution.

Many academic journals are peer reviewed. This process involves submitted articles being sent out to subject specialists for comment prior to publication. It is this process that enables readers to have faith in the academic reliability of an article. Researchers should be aware whether or not the journals they use are peer reviewed, and this should be taken into account in their evaluation of the validity of the content.

Conference Papers

Publications relating to a conference, convention, or symposium may include pre-prints, proceedings, and conference records. These publications can be called grey literature (see below).

Pre-prints are often published before or in time for the event and can be a valuable record of work currently in progress. The papers are reviewed following the event and published as conference proceedings or transactions. Because conference speakers deliver papers concerning their current work, they are a vital resource for researchers wishing to remain up to date with activities in their chosen subject area. Depending on the organization arranging the conference, proceedings may be made available shortly after the event and easy to access. Sadly, this is not always the case as some papers are not published until a long period has lapsed and others are only available at the event itself.

Because of these problems and the fact that no bibliographic records may exist, conference papers can be difficult to obtain. The publisher is often a professional body such as the IEEE (Institute of Electrical and Electronics Engineers), the AES (Audio Engineering Society), the BMA (British Medical Association), or the Royal Historical Society and not a large publishing house.

Searching conference proceedings is made possible by indexes such as the *Conference Papers Index* (provided by Cambridge Scientific Abstracts), *Index to Scientific and Technical Proceedings* (from ISI Web of Knowledge), and the British Library's ZETOC[1] service. Many of the indexes are published electronically. Details of the author and title of a paper can sometimes be found by seeking out the conference website.

Manuscripts and incunabula

Manuscripts can include items such as letters, manuscripts of poems and novels, notebooks, and diaries. Incunabula are early printed books, generally prior to the sixteenth century. All of these items may be difficult to trace and access. The British Library has an early printed collection and an incunabula short title catalogue (ISTC) which includes locations from around the world. The key to finding these items can be to identify collections which contain holdings in a relevant subject area. Because of their nature, access may be restricted. Collections that hold such materials will probably include archives, private collections, collections of learned societies, and so on.

Grey literature and ephemera

Grey literature comprises those publications that are not easily identified nor accessed via the usual sources such as booksellers. Types of grey literature include:

- conference proceedings (see above)
- theses
- company reports
- some official publications
- research papers prior to publication
- local records

These types of publications do not usually have a linked bibliographic description or an ISBN, and this lack of information means that they can be difficult to obtain.

Ephemera are those publications which are often disposable or single sheets that would not be considered minor publications. The *Concise Oxford Dictionary* defines the word ephemeral as 'lasting or of use for only a short time; transitory' (Allen 1991: 393). Because of this there are difficulties in both identifying and accessing these materials. Although not scholarly documents, they can form a vital part of a researcher's information resources. Ephemera may include:

- pamphlets
- leaflets such as marketing or promotional materials
- forms

There are often no records that they have been produced at all, especially in the public domain. Ephemeral publications may be a 'one-off' with no remaining copies.

In more recent years, libraries have become aware of the lack of information and holdings of these materials and open access repositories are paving the way for their improved access and storage. One example of ephemera being made more widely available is the JISC-funded digitization of selections from the John Johnson Collection (items date between 1508 and 1939) at the University of Oxford.

Publishers of these documents may be anyone from a large organization, a government body, a commercial company, or an individual. The majority of ephemeral documents may be lost. Many are supplied free of charge while some may only be available internally to members of an organization.

Maps and charts

The range of maps and charts is vast and libraries may be selective about the collection they retain. Storage can be difficult: large maps require large flat drawers, atlases can be oversized and difficult to handle and historical maps may need special archival conditions. Currency can be imperative in certain situations, but historical data is of equal value in others. Maps can be made using a variety of criteria and the researcher may need to consider any or all of the following variables:

- Date
- Scale
- Topographical subject matter
- Geological subject matter
- Land use subject matter
- Atlases (road atlas, demographic, historical, and so on)
- Whether or not the map was created by a national survey organization

Difficulties might be encountered when attempting to locate and access foreign and historical maps. Atlases may contain an index which guides the searcher to particular page and map reference, but maps do not usually have this information.

Cataloguers should follow the guidelines for cartographic materials, but this is dependent on the skill of the cataloguer. Researchers should be prepared for some lateral thinking when searching catalogues for maps and charts.

Maps may be produced by a national survey organization such as the Ordnance Survey (Ordnance Survey 2004) in the UK, specialist institutes such as the British Geological Society or commercial publishers, then stored in specialist libraries such as that at the Royal Geographical Society.[2] They are increasingly being made available in a digital format (for example, by the British Geological Survey[3]) and users should be aware of different data storage, for example, raster images and vector data and whether specialist software such as a GIS (Geographical Information System) is required. Specialist maps may be expensive.

Microforms

- Microfilm, microfiche, and microprint (and microcard) are all types of microform. Each is a means of storing an image of a document in a reduced version.
- Microfiche is a 15cm by 10cm (6 inches by 4 inches) sheet of film that can hold up to about 100 pages at 24 times reduction.
- Microfilm comes in two sizes: 16mm and 35mm.
- Microprint (and microcard) is less common. The image is stored on a stiff card.

Micro storage formats are relatively cheap to produce and are expected to be long-lasting, so are still a popular choice for documents such as rare items which should not be handled, those in a bad state of repair, and those with a limited print run. Because of the low cost, they are sometimes used for indexes and other records that need to be kept up to date and therefore frequently produced. An additional benefit for the library or organization is that of storage: microforms take up very little space.

All these forms necessitate the use of a special reader to enable the user to view the information. Many libraries possess a microfilm/microfiche/microprint reader and some also have the extra facility of a reader/printer for printing copies of the document(s). Like photocopying, there is likely to be a charge for this service. These machines are straightforward to operate, although it can be a challenge loading a microfilm in the correct orientation if a previous user has wound the film on the spool incorrectly. As with computer visual display units (VDUs), it is difficult to read large amounts of material on a screen. Because they are an image rather than computer readable data, searching involves use of an index (if it exists).

Items that are likely to be stored in microform are:

- Newspapers (for example, the British Library Newspaper collection)
- Books (the Library of Congress[4] has a large collection)
- Rare or historic documents (for example, medieval manuscripts, author's original manuscripts, notebooks, or correspondence)
- Indexes and bibliographies
- Historical records or historical and genealogical society information
- Many other primary sources of information (for example, parliamentary papers and cabinet minutes)
- Theses and **dissertations** (as held by the British Library Document Supply Centre)

Although many libraries house microform collections, users need to be aware of how these items are indicated on the catalogue. The RSLG (Research Support Libraries Group) ran a survey of microforms in UK HE institutions. They concluded that 'it is clear from this survey that records for these kinds of material are imperfect and inconsistent. As a class they can not uniformly be retrieved through OPACs' (Feather 1999: 17).

Many research libraries hold microforms and corresponding readers. The British Library and the Library of Congress have extensive collections of microform materials.

Electronic (not including audio and visual materials)

The general electronic formats referred to here include:

- Web-based/online resources
- CD-ROMs
- Formats such as PDF (portable document format), word processing, spread-sheets, and databases
- Floppy disk
- Electronic versions of print formats (for example, e-journals)

Electronic formats of information sources have a number of benefits:

- They can be kept up to date, particularly when Web-based, sometimes to the hour (for example, legal databases such as Westlaw from Sweet and Maxwell are updated three times per day so that users have access to the most recent information)
- Many can be accessed from anywhere in the world with suitable equipment and authentication
- Flexible searching of content
- They take up minimal if any physical storage space (apart from the necessary hardware)
- Additional data, multimedia sources, and appropriate websites can be accessed directly from the content via a link

However, the situation is not always as rosy as it may at first seem. Internet-based resources can be current, but this relies on the publisher updating regularly. If a problem with currency is identified, the user may lose faith in its reliability. CD-ROMs may only be updated monthly, or even quarterly. They are therefore not always particularly current, especially towards the end of the current period.

Many electronic formats are designed to be intuitive and easy to use, even for the unfamiliar user. Interfaces vary from those that guide the user step by step, to those that are complex for the new user. There are sometimes confusing quirks regarding usage. A member of library staff will help in the use of electronic resources.

The accessibility of electronic resources is dependent on three factors:

- Authentication and authorization
- Location (for IP (internet protocol) authentication)
- Hardware and software

Although some electronic resources are freely available (for example, services such as Intute,[5] others require authentication, usually in the form of a user-name and password. Without the appropriate authentication, the user is unable to access the resource (see Chapter 2). An Internet-based resource is often available from anywhere in the world with Internet access. Those that restrict use by using IP address as authentication will only be available from computers having those addresses. Often CD-ROM resources are only available on a network in a particular location.

One of the real benefits of electronic resources is the ability to search the entire content. The success of this depends on the skill of the user and the construction of the resource. Some resources offer only a basic search facility while others allow for detailed, structured searching. Users should be aware of the maxim 'rubbish in, rubbish out', and search with care.

As with hardcopy materials, the bibliographic records of electronic resources vary. Users often experience difficulties when attempting to reference electronic sources (see Chapter 12): this is a result of them being unsure which information needs to be included and/or a lack of the information required.

Electronic formats such as CD-ROMs and DVDs have not been in existence long enough to prove their longevity. Since CDs only came on the market in 1982, it has yet to be proven whether or not they will retain all the data stored on them in a readable form for long-term storage. Another major problem is that of retaining the hardware or the programs to be able to read the files. It is likely that DVD format will be superseded by another format not yet invented. Libraries often retain copies of resources in a format on which they believe they can rely, which may explain why microform is still going strong.

Audio visual formats

Since Thomas Edison applied for the patent of his wax phonograph in 1877 there have been a host of developments in the devices designed to store audio. The same is true of the means of recording and storing images, both still and moving. A huge leap was made with the dawn of the digital era. This gave rise to many of the devices that are in common use today.

Currency is not generally an issue in audio visual recordings as they are usually the record of an event or performance at a specific point in time or of a work of art.

Audio visual items often form specialist collections, for example, the National Sound Archive (at the British Library). As is the case with printed items, rare and historic items can be difficult to obtain or access.

The search facility of audio or moving image recordings can be a problem. If a modern recording has some form of timecode built in which the searcher is able to use, and they know the point they wish to access, all is well and good. A score may aid a search of a music recording, but other than that, it relies on the searcher's knowledge and patience. Still images may form part of a volume with an index which can be used to locate a particular image.

Provided adequate care is taken, the lifespan of a vinyl disc, film, or photograph may be extremely long (although there has not been the opportunity to test these formats over more than a century or so). As with other electronic resources, the case of digital recordings is as yet unknown. And similarly, reproduction relies on suitable equipment being available.

Some of the older formats may be transferred to a more modern system (for example, a cinefilm may be transferred to video or DVD). If this is the case, the modern format may be easily accessible and the original remain in ideal conditions in an archive.

The cost of these items is the price charged for obtaining a copy. For example, the National Sound Archive charges by the hour (copies are made in real time). Quality diminishes with each subsequent copy made, although modern transcription techniques make this less of a problem. Any copies made by the researcher should comply with current copyright law.

The publisher of an audio visual item may not always be obvious. Commercial recordings have the identity of the publisher on the packaging and/or the item itself, but identification of the publisher of an obscure item may present problems.

A library stocking any audiovisual formats may also provide the means for playing them. A user might be able to manipulate the controls expertly on a MP3 player, but not be so confident in how to operate a reel to reel tape recorder or vinyl disc player. There should be a member of staff available to help the user with equipment use.

A single item, such as a CD or vinyl disc may contain the recordings of a number of works. The full contents are not always included in the catalogue record, so a searcher looking for a recording of Chopin's Fantaisie-Impromptu, *Opus 66* may not discover a recording on a disc with the title *Great Pianists of the 20th Century: Artur Rubenstein* (Rubinstein 1998).

Artefacts

An artefact could be almost anything and libraries may contain a selection, although some items are more likely to be housed in a museum. The researcher in pursuit of artefacts will need to search for the details to locate the item, for example, in a museum or library catalogue. The catalogue records should contain descriptive information and may contain a photograph of the item.

Artefacts can include a vast array of forms such as:

- specimens (geological, medical, etc.)
- toys

* tools
* teaching materials (for example, those used in an infant school)

Researchers may need to obtain special permission to access and handle items and it is likely they will have to travel to the library or museum.

People

One must not overlook this valuable form of information storage. Whether it is an expert in the chosen subject, a colleague, or members of the public, researchers often tap into the knowledge (or opinions) of others. Eliciting information may take care and persistence and the researcher will need some form of storage for the information gathered. This could be in the form of an audio recording, notes taken during an interview, a questionnaire and so on.

Key points

* Be familiar with the benefits and drawbacks of the formats used
* Be aware of the difficulties of accessing some formats and plan the research accordingly

---

Glossary

Abstract A summary of an article

Appropriate copy The version of an item which is most appropriate to the context of the user

Athens An authentication service used to validate the eligibility of the user to access a resource. Many information providers allow Athens authentication

Boolean operators (or connectors) a means of using the principle of logic devised by a nineteenth century mathematician: AND, OR, and NOT

Call number A number assigned to each item so that it may be retrieved (see also classification number and shelfmark

Catalogue A list of all the library's holdings. May be printed or available online

Catalogue record The information about a work stored on a catalogue

Classification system A means of organizing items by subject, keeping like subjects together

Classification number A number assigned to each item, determined by a classification schedule and enabling orderly shelving and retrieval. See also call number and shelfmark

Closed access When items are stored so they are not accessible by users. Items are requested by users and fetched for them by library staff

Collection A collective term for the holdings of a library. One library may have many discrete collections

Concurrent users The number of people using the same resource at the same time

Digital repository *See* repository

Dissertation A publication forming a requirement for an academic taught course

Document delivery/supply The supply of documents from a remote source

e-book An electronic version or edition of a book which could be a scanned copy of a print version or a born-digital publication

e-print Usually an electronic version of a journal article. It can be a pre-print (before being refereed) or a post-print (having been refereed and including any changes from that process)

Electronic resource Any information supplied electronically. Typical resources include e-journals, online databases, and CD-ROMs

Ephemera Publications such as leaflets or forms which are not formally published and have no bibliographic record at the time of publication

Freely available   At no monetary cost to the user and with no authentication required

Grey literature   Publications that are not created and made available via formal means and therefore have no bibliographic record when published. Include theses and conference proceedings

Interlibrary loan   A means of obtaining items not held at the home library

Item   A single manifestation of a work

Licence   An agreement between the user (or more commonly the institution) and the supplier of a service (usually an electronic resource). Conditions of use form part of the licence

Loan entitlement   The numbers of items that a user is permitted to borrow and the length of time for which they may retain those items

Microform   A format that requires magnification to be able to see the content

Open access   Items that the library user may access for themselves on open shelves or electronic resources available without barrier to access

Query   The term(s) used for searching

Repository   An electronic store of research output (usually) including pre-prints, post-prints, bibliographic information, and other materials. May be open access

Serial   A publication that is issued in successive, numbered (or chronological) parts with no set end date

Shelfmark   The numbers and/or letters assigned to each item so it may be retrieved. May include other characters as well as the classmark. See also classmark and call number

Stopword   A word in common usage that a search function will not allow or will ignore as it would produce too many results. For example: the, of, for, that

Subscription   A fee paid for a service or resource, usually for a designated period of time

Thesis   A publication resulting from doctoral research and submitted in fulfilment of the award of PhD (or similar)

Work   A manifestation of an author's/creator's output for example, *War and Peace* by Trollope or *Pictures at an Exhibition* by Mussorgsky

References and bibliography

Note: All URLs checked 8/9 July 2007.

Abbott, D. (2003) Overcoming the dangers of technical obsolescence: rescuing the BBC Domesday project, *Digicult.Info*, August, 4: 7–10. Available at: www.digicult.info/pages/newsletter.php

Alkire, L.G. (ed.) (2006) *Periodical Title Abbreviations*, 17th edn. London: Thomson Gale.

Allen, R.E. (ed.) (1991) *The Concise Oxford Dictionary*, 8th edn. Oxford: Oxford University Press.

Andrew, T. (2003) Trends in self-posting of research material online by academic staff, *Ariadne*, 30 October, 37. UKOLN: Bath. Available at: www.ariadne.ac.uk/issue37/andrew/

Armstrong, C.J., Lonsdale, R.E., Stoker, D.A., and Urquhart, C.J. (2000) *Final Report – 1999/2000 Cycle*, JUSTEIS JISC Usage Surveys, Trends in Electronic Information Services, August. Aberystwyth: Department of Information Studies, University of Wales. Available at: www.dil.aber.ac.uk/dils/research/justeis/cyc1rep0.htm

BBSRC (2006) *BBSRC's Position on Deposit of Publications*. Swindon: Biotechnology and Biological Sciences Research Council. Available at: www.bbsrc.ac.uk/news/articles/28_june_research_access.html

BBSRC (2007) *Areas of Science*. Swindon: Biotechnology and Biological Sciences Research Council. Available at: www.bbsrc.ac.uk/science/areas/Welcome.html

Berman, F., Fox, G., and Hey, T. (eds) (2003) *Grid Computing: Making the Global Infrastructure a Reality*. Chichester: John Wiley & Sons Ltd. Available at: www.wileyeurope.com/WileyCDA/WileyTitle/productCd-0470853190.html

Berners-Lee, T., Hendler, J., and Lassila, O. (2001) The semantic Web: a new form of Web content that is meaningful to computers will unleash a revolution of new possibilities, *Scientific American*, May. Available at: www.sciam.com/article.cfm?articleID=00048144-10D2-1C70-84A9809EC588EF21&pageNumber=1&catID=2

BioMed Central (2004) *What is BioMed Central?* London: BioMed Central. Available at: www.biomedcentral.com/info/

BOAI (2007) *Budapest Open Access Initiative: Frequently Asked Questions*. Budapest: BOAI. Available at: www.earlham.edu/~peters/fos/boaifaq.htm#openaccess

Bradley, P. (2004) *Phil Bradley's website*. Available at: www.philb.com/

Bradley, P. (2008) *Phil Bradley's website. Phil Bradley, Internet Consultant*. Available at http://www.philb.com/

British Library (2004) *Reader Admissions*. London: British Library. Available at: www.bl.uk/services/reading/admissions.html

BSI (British Standards Institution) (1989) *Recommendations for References to Published Materials*, BS 1629: 1989. London: BSI.

BSI (British Standards Institution) (1990) *Recommendations for Citing and Referencing Published Material*, BS 5605: 1990. London: BSI.

Buzan, T. (2006) *Mind Mapping: Kickstart Your Creativity and Transform Your Life*. London: BBC Active.

Carroll, J. (2002) *A Handbook for Deterring Plagiarism in Higher Education*. Oxford: Oxford Brookes University.

Carroll, J. (2003) *Plagiarism: Is There a Virtual Solution?* (Based on an exercise in Academic Writing for Graduate Students by Swales and Feale, University of Michigan, 1993). Oxford: Oxford Centre for Staff and Learning Development, Oxford Brookes University. Available at: www.brookes.ac.uk/services/ocsd/2_learntch/plagiarism.html

CLA (Copyright Licensing Agency) (2007) *List of Excluded Categories and Excluded Works*. London: Copyright Licensing Agency. Available at: www.cla.co.uk/support/excluded.html

Connotea (2007) *About Connotea*. Available at: www.connotea.org/about

Creative Commons (2007) *About Us. 'Some Rights Reserved': Building a Layer of Reasonable Copyright*. Stanford, CA: Creative Commons. Available at: //creativecommons.org/learn/aboutus/

CURL (Consortium of University Research Libraries) (2003) *CURL Membership and Partnership Guidelines: Guidelines for Membership*. Available at: www.curl.ac.uk/members/guidelines.htm

Day, M. (2003) Prospects for institutional e-print repositories in the United Kingdom, *ePrints UK Supporting Study, No. 1*. Bath: UKOLN. Available at: www.rdn.ac.uk/projects/eprints-uk/docs/studies/impact/

DCC (2007a) *About the DCC*. Edinburgh: Digital Curation Centre. Available at: www.dcc.ac.uk/about/

DCC (2007b) *Welcome*. Edinburgh: Digital Curation Centre. Available at: www.dcc.ac.uk/

DOAJ (Directory of Open Access Journals) (2007) *About: Definitions*. Available at: www.doaj.org/

Dobratz, S. and Mattaei, B. (2003) Open archives activities and experiences in Europe: an overview by the Open Archives Forum, *D-Lib Magazine*, January, 9(1). Available at: www.dlib.org/dlib/january03/dobratz/01dobratz.html

DoH (Department of Health) and HMPS (Her Majesty's Prison Service) (2003) *A Pharmacy Service for Prisoners*, Prison Health Report. London: Department of Health. Available at: www.dh.gov.uk/assetRoot/04/06/57/07/04065707.pdf

DoH (Department of Health) (2007) *The National Research Register*. London: Department of Health. Available at: www.nrr.nhs.uk/

Dolphin, I., Miller, P., and Sherratt, R. (2002) Portals, portals everywhere, *Ariadne*, October, 33. Available at: www.ariadne.ac.uk/issue33/portals/

DPC (Digital Preservation Coalition) (2002) *Welcome to the Digital Preservation Coalition Website*. London: Digital Preservation Coalition. Available at: www.dpconline.org/graphics/index.html

e-Science (2004) *e-Science and Grid Definitions*. London: Department of Trade and Industry and the UK Research Councils, HMSO. Available at: www.escience-grid.org.uk/docs/gridtech/define.htm

ESRC (Economic and Social Research Council) (2007) *What is ESRC Society Today?* Swindon: ESRC.

EU (European Union) (2007a) Scientific information in the digital age: access, dissemination and preservation, SEC (2007)181. COM (2007) 56, final. Available at: http://ec.europa.eu/research/science-society/page_en.cfm?id=3184

EU (European Union) (2007b) *Official Journal of the European Union*, EU Publications Office. Available at: http://publications.europa.eu/official/index_en.htm

European Library, The (2007) Available at: www.theeuropeanlibrary.org/portal/index.html

Expert Information (2007) *Index to Theses*. London: Expert Information. Available at: www.theses.com/

Feather, J. (1999) *Survey of Microform Sets: A Report for Research Support Libraries Programme*. Available at: www.rslp.ac.uk/Studies/Feather.doc

Fisher, D. and Hanstock, T. (2003) *Citing References: A Guide for Users*, 5th edn. Nottingham: Nottingham Trent University. Available at: www2.ntu.ac.uk/llr/library/citingrefs.htm

Gadd, E., Oppenheim, C., and Probets, S. (2003) RoMEO Studies 1: The impact of copyright ownership on academic author self-archiving, *Journal of Documentation*, 59(3): 243–77. Available at: www.lboro.ac.uk/departments/ls/disresearch/romeo/Romeo%20Deliverables.htm

Granger, S. (2000) Emulation as a digital preservation strategy, *D-Lib Magazine* October, 6(10). Available at: www.dlib.org/dlib/october00/granger/10granger.html

Harnad, S. (2001) For whom the gate tolls? How and why to free the refereed research literature online through author/institution self-archiving, now, *ECS, Electronics and Computer Science*. Southampton: University of Southampton. Available at: http://eprints.ecs.soton.ac.uk/8705/.

Harnad, S. (2003) Open access to peer-reviewed research through author/institution self-archiving: maximizing research impact by maximizing online access, in D. Law and J. Andrews (eds), *Digital Libraries: Policy Planning and Practice*. Aldershot: Ashgate Publishing.

Hawkins, L. and Hirons, J. (2002) Transforming AACR2: using the revised rules in Chapters 9 and 12, workshop presentation at NASIG (North American Serials Interest Group) 17th Annual conference. Transforming Serials: The Revolution Continues, Williamsburg, VA, 20–3 June. Available at: www.loc.gov/acq/conser/

Hey, T. and Trefethen, A. (2003) *The Data Deluge: An e-Science Perspective*. Available at: www.rcuk.ac.uk/cmsweb/downloads/rcuk/research/esci/datadeluge.pdf

HMSO (Her Majesty's Stationery Office) (2003) *Access to Information*. London: HMSO. Available at: www.hmso.gov.uk/information/access_information.htm

Hodgson, K. (2002) Vulcan crosswords and dodgy deadlines, *Academic News*, Autumn. Available at: www.smlawpub.co.uk/academic/acad02.pdf

IALS (Institute of Advanced Legal Studies) (2002) *Current Legal Research Topics Database Project*. London: Institute of Advanced Legal Studies, University of London. Available at: http://ials.sas.ac.uk/library/clrt/clrt.htm

IFLA (International Federation of Library Associations and Institutions) (2005) *Library & Information Science: Style Guides for Electronic Resources*. The Hague: IFLA. Available at: www.ifla.org/I/training/citation/citing.htm

Information Services, Cardiff University (2004) *Cardiff Index to Legal Abbreviations*. Cardiff: Cardiff University Information Services. Available at: www.legalabbrevs.cardiff.ac.uk

Intute (2006) *Intute*. Manchester: The Intute Consortium. Available at: www.intute.ac.uk/

JISC (Joint Information Systems Committee) (2004) *Investing in the Future: Developing an Online Information Environment*. London: JISC. Available at: www.jisc.ac.uk/index.cfm?name=ie_home

JISC (Joint Information Systems Committee) (2007a) *Portals: Frequently Asked Questions*.

London: JISC. Available at: www.jisc.ac.uk/whatwedo/programmes/programme_portals/ie_portalsfaq.aspx

JISC (Joint Information Systems Committee) (2007b) *What We Do: e-Research*. London: JISC. Available at: www.jisc.ac.uk/whatwedo/themes/eresearch.aspx

JISC (Joint Information Systems Committee) (2007c) *What We Do: Programmes*. London: JISC. Available at: www.jisc.ac.uk/whatwedo/programmes.aspx

Johnston, W. (2003) The concept of plagiarism, *Learning & Teaching in Action*, 2(1). Available at: www.ltu.mmu.ac.ltia/issue4/johnston.shtml

Lawrence, S., Giles, C.L., and Bollacker, K. (1999) Digital libraries and autonomous citation indexing, *IEEE Computer*, 32(6): 67–71.

Legal Deposit Libraries Act 2003, c. 28. HMSO: London. Available at: www.opsi.gov.uk/acts/acts2003/20030028.htm

Lieb, R. (ed.) (2007) *Search Engine Watch*. London: Incisive Interactive Marketing LLC. Available at: www.searchenginewatch.com/

LSE (London School of Economics) (2007) *The Library*. London: British Library of Political and Economic Science. Available at: www.lse.ac.uk/library/

Lyon, L. (2003) eBank UK: building the links between research data, scholarly communication and learning, *Ariadne*, July, 36. Available at: www.ariadne.ac.uk/issue36/lyon/

MacColl, J. (2006) Google challenges for academic libraries, *Ariadne*, February, 46. Available at: www.ariadne.ac.uk/issue46/maccoll/intro.html

McKiernan, G. (2004) *All that JAS: Journal Abbreviation Sources*. Iowa: Iowa State University. Available at: www2.iastate.edu/~CYBERSTACKS/JAS.htm

MRC (Medical Research Council) (2006) *MRC Guidance on Open Access to Published Research*. London: Medical Research Council. Available at: www.mrc.ac.uk/Policy-Guidance/EthicsAndGovernance/OpenAccessPublishingandArchiving/MRCGuideforResearchersonOpenAccessPublishing/index.htm

NaCTeM (National Centre for Text Mining) (2007) *Frequently Asked Questions: What is Text Mining?* Manchester: National Centre for Text Mining, University of Manchester. Available at: www.nactem.ac.uk/

National Archives (2007) *ARCHON Directory*. Kew: The National Archives. Available at: www.nationalarchives.gov.uk/archon/

National e-Science Centre (2007) *Defining e-Science*. Edinburgh: National e-Science Centre. Available at: www.nesc.ac.uk/nesc/define.html

Notess, G. (2007) *SearchEngineShowdown: The User's Guide to Web Searching*. Available at: http://searchengineshowdown.com/

Office of Scientific and Technical Information (2007) *GrayLIT Network. About*. Oak Ridge: Office of Scientific and Technical Information. Available at: www.osti.gov/graylit/about.html

ONS (Office for National Statistics) (2007) *National Statistics*. Newport: ONS. Available at: www.statistics.gov.uk/

OPSI (Office of Public Sector Information) (2007) Home page, *Unlocking the Potential of Public Sector Information*. London: Office of Public Sector Information. Available at: www.opsi.gov.uk/

Ordnance Survey (2004) *Site Home Page*. Southampton: Ordnance Survey. Available at: www.ordnancesurvey.co.uk/oswebsite/

Orna, E. with Stevens, G. (2000) *Managing Information for Research*. Buckingham: Open University Press.

Palgrave Macmillan (2007) *The Grants Register*. Basingstoke: Palgrave Macmillan.

Paskin, N. (2003) DOI: a 2003 progress report, *D-Lib Magazine*, June, 9(6). Available at: www.dlib.org/dlib/june03/paskin/06paskin.html

Place, E., Kendall, M., Hiom, D. et al. (2006) Press release. Internet Detective – back on the case, 13 June, *Internet Detective: Wise Up to the Web*, 3rd edn. Available at: www.vts.intute.ac.uk/detective/

PLoS (Public Library of Science) (2007) *About PLoS: Missions and Goals*. Available at: www.plos.org/about/index.html

Raistrick, D. (1993) *Index to Legal Citations and Abbreviations*, 2nd edn. London: Bowker-Saur.

RCUK (Research Councils UK) (2002) *e-Science Core Programme Welcome: First Phase of the Programme*. Swindon: RCUK. Available at: www.rcuk.ac.uk/escience/default.htm

RCUK (Research Council UK) (2006) *Research Councils UK Publishes Update of Position Statement on Access to Research Outputs*. Swindon: RCUK. Available at: www.rcuk.ac.uk/aboutrcuk/publications/policy/20060628openaccess.htm

RCUK (Research Councils UK) (2007) *Welcome to Research Councils UK*. Swindon: RCUK. Available at: www.rcuk.ac.uk/

Reynard, K.W. (ed.) (2004) *Aslib Directory of Information Sources in the United Kingdom*, 13th edn. London: Routledge.

Richards, M.P. (2002). *The Evolution of Hominid Dietary Adaptations Linked with Environmental Changes: Extending the Record Beyond 100,000 Years*. London: Funding Council Research Grant, NERC. Available at: www.nerc.ac.uk/research/programmes/efched/results/richards.asp

RIN (Research Information Network) (2007) *About the Research Information Network*. London: Research Information Network. Available at: www.rin.ac.uk/about

RSLG (Research Support Libraries Group) (2003) Paragraphs 42 and 64, *Final Report*. London: HEFCE (Higher Education Funding Council for England). Available at: www.rslg.ac.uk/final/final.pdf

Rubinstein, A. (1998) CD recording of Chopin: Fantaisie-Impromptu in C Sharp Minor, Opus 66, *Great Pianists of the 20th Century*, Philips Classics 456 955–2, track 5, first recorded 1964.

SARA (Scholarly Articles Research Alerting) (2004) *Scholarly Articles Research Alerting*. London: Taylor & Francis. Available at: www.tandf.co.uk/sara/

SCIE (Social Care Institute for Excellence) (2007) *National Research Register for Social Care – About*. London: Social Care Institute for Excellence. Available at: www.scie-socialcareonline.org.uk/researchRegister/about.asp

Sharp, J.A., and Peters, J., and Howard, K. (2002) *The Management of a Student Research Project*, 3rd edn. Aldershot: Gower.

Simpson, P. (2002) E-Prints and the Open Archive Initiative – Opportunities for Libraries, in J.W. Markham (ed.), *IAMSLIC 2002 Conference Proceedings Bridging the Digital Divide, Mazatlan, Sinaloa, Mexico, 6–11 October*. Available at: http://tardis.eprints.org/papers/

Shoemaker, D. (2000) *Theories of Delinquency: An Examination of Explanations of Delinquent Behaviour*. Oxford: Oxford University Press.

SPARC Europe (2007) Available at: www.sparceurope.org/

SUNCAT (2007) *Description of SUNCAT*. Edinburgh: EDINA. Available at: www.suncat.ac.uk/description.shtml

TSO (The Stationery Office) (2007) *UKOP the Home of Official Publications*. Available at: www.ukop.co.uk/

Turner, P. and Elmes, H. (eds) (2006) *Commonwealth Universities Yearbook*, 80th edn. London: Association of Commonwealth Universities.

UK-IPO (UK Intellectual Property Office) (2003a) *Copyright: What is Copyright?* Newport: UK-IPO. Available at: www.ipo.gov.uk/whatis/whatis-copy.htm

UK-IPO (UK Intellectual Property Office) (2003b) *Trademarks: What is a Trademark?* Newport: UK-IPO. Available at: www.ipo.gov.uk/whatis/whatis-tm.htm

UK-IPO (UK Intellectual Property Office) (2003c) *Designs: What is a Design?* Newport: UK-IPO. Available at: www.ipo.gov.uk/whatis/whatis-design.htm

Van de Sompel, H. and Beit-Arie, O. (2001) Open linking in the scholarly information environment using the OpenURL framework, *D-Lib Magazine*, 7(3). Available at: www.dlib.org/dlib/march01/vandesompel/03vandesompel.html#fig1

Wang, E. (1995) Studies on the genomes of wild-type and vaccine strains of yellow fever virus, unpublished PhD thesis, University of Surrey.

Wellcome Trust (2007a) Wellcome Library, *About Us*. London: Wellcome Trust. Available at: http://library.wellcome.ac.uk/about.html

Wellcome Trust (2007b) *Wellcome Trust Position Statement in Support of Open and Unrestricted Access to Published Research*, 14 March. London: Wellcome Trust. Available at: www.wellcome.ac.uk/doc_wtd002766.html

West, C. (2002) Reactions to the Research Support Libraries Group: a view from Wales, *The New Review of Academic Librarianship*, 8: 139–51. (Note: the date of the publication is correct even though the date of publication of the report is February 2003 – see the journal editor's introduction)

Woldering, B. (2003) *The European Library (TEL) – The Gate to Europe's Knowledge*. Available at: www.europeanlibrary.org/

Web addresses

Note: all addresses were accessed on 8/9 July 2007.

Chapter 2

1 HERO: www.hero.ac.uk/
2 M25 Consortium: www.m25lib.ac.uk/Guide/directory
3 COPAC: www.copac.ac.uk/
4 The British Library: www.bl.uk/
5 Bodleian Library, Oxford: www.bodley.ox.ac.uk/
6 National Library of Scotland, Edinburgh: www.nls.uk/
7 National Library of Wales, Aberystwyth: www.llgc.org.uk/
8 Trinity College Library, Dublin: www.tcd.ie/Library/
9 University Library, Cambridge: www.lib.cam.ac.uk/
10 Researcher's Gateway: www.surrey.ac.uk/Library/

Chapter 3

1 COS: www.cos.com/
2 CORDIS: www.cordis.lu/en/home.html
3 PhDData: www.phddata.org
4 NHS National Research Register: www.nrr.nhs.uk/
5 Oasis: oasis.bbsrc.ac.uk/Welcome.html
6 HERO: www.hero.ac.uk/
7 British Thesis Service: www.bl.uk/britishthesis/
8 UMI Digital Dissertations: wwwlib.umi.com/dissertations/

Chapter 5

1 CrossRef: www.crossref.org/
2 IngentaConnect: www.ingentaconnect.com/
3 APA (American Psychological Association): www.apa.org/
4 National Art Library: www.vam.ac.uk/nal/
5 National Electronic Library for Health: www.nelh.nhs.uk/
6 National Electronic Library for Mental Health: www.nelmh.org/
7 BFI National Library: www.bfi.org.uk/nationallibrary/
8 IALS Library: http://ials.sas.ac.uk/library/library.htm
9 The Courtauld Institute of Art library (also available via COPAC): www.courtauld.ac.uk
10 Institute of Electrical Engineers: www.iee.org/TheIEE/Research/LibSvc/index.cfm

11 RIBA (Royal Institute of British Architects) British Architectural Library: www.architecture.com/go/Architecture/Reference/Library_898.html
12 London Mathematical Society: www.lms.ac.uk/
13 Natural History Museum Library: www.nhm.ac.uk/library/index.html
14 Royal Horticultural Society: www.rhs.org.uk/libraries/index.asp
15 National Oceanographic Library: www.soc.soton.ac.uk/LIB/
16 Centre for Ecology and Hydrology: www.ceh.ac.uk/
17 The Royal Society of Chemistry: www.rsc.org/lic/library.htm
18 The Royal Society: www.royalsoc.ac.uk/
19 The Women's library: www.thewomenslibrary.ac.uk/
20 London Business School Library Service: www.london.edu/library.html
21 WiLL: www.londonlibraries.org.uk/will/
22 OAIster: www.oaister.org/
23 BUFVC: www.bufvc.ac.uk/
24 Education Image Gallery (EIG): http://edina.ac.uk/eig
25 ZETOC: http://zetoc.mimas.ac.uk/
26 New York Public Library: www.nypl.org/
27 BOPCRIS: www.bopcris.ac.uk/
28 UK National Archives: www.nationalarchives.gov.uk/

Chapter 7

1 UK Intellectual Property Office Patent: www.patent.gov.uk/patent.htm
2 US Patent Office, Patent Full-Text and Full-Page Image Database: www.uspto.gov/patft/index.html
3 British Standards: www.bsi.org.uk

Chapter 8

1 Archives Hub: www.archiveshub.ac.uk/
2 Backstage: www.backstage.ac.uk/
3 SUNCAT: www.suncat.ac.uk/
4 COPAC: http://copac.ac.uk/
5 CAIRNS: http://cairns.lib.strath.ac.uk
6 SALSER: http://edina.ed.ac.uk/salser
7 M25 ULS: www.m25lib.ac.uk/ULS/
8 Directory of Open Access Journals (DAOJ): www.doaj.org/
9 RePEc: http://repec.org/
10 OAIster: http://oaister.umdl.umich.edu/o/oaister/
11 AbeBooks: www.abebooks.com/
12 Bookfinder: www.bookfinder.com/
13 European Information Network in the UK: www.europe.org.uk
14 UK National Register of Archives (NRA): www.nationalarchives.gov.uk/nra/
15 Archives Hub: www.archiveshub.ac.uk/
16 Access to Archives (A2A): www.a2a.org.uk/
17 SCONE (Scottish Collections Network Extension): http://scone.strath.ac.uk/
18 AIM25: www.aim25.ac.uk/

Chapter 9

1 Wikipedia: www.wikipedia.org/
2 Northern Light: www.northernlight.com/
3 Alta Vista: http://uk.altavista.com/
4 All the Web: www.alltheweb.com/
5 Yahoo Search Directory: http://dir.yahoo.com/
6 Ixquick: www.ixquick.com/
7 Kartoo: www.kartoo.com/
8 Lycos Français: www.lycos.fr/
9 WWW.Fi: http://www.fi/
10 Google Scholar: http://scholar.google.com/
11 Windows Live Academic Search: http://academic.live.com
12 Google UK: www.google.co.uk
13 Ask.com: http://uk.ask.com/
14 Clusty: http://clusty.com/
15 Scirus: www.scirus.com/
16 International Directory of Search Engines: www.searchenginecolossus.com/

Chapter 10

1 Project Gutenberg: www.gutenberg.net/index.shtml
2 SCONUL Research Extra: www.sconul.ac.uk/using_other_libraries/srx/
3 British Library Document Supply: www.bl.uk/services/document/dsc.html
4 DocDel/Instant Information Systems: www.docdel.com/
5 Kluwer: www.wkap.nl/journal/
6 Science Direct: www.sciencedirect.com/
7 arXiv: http://arXiv.org
8 RePEc (Research Papers in Economics): http://repec.org/
9 E-print network: www.osti.gov/eprints/
10 OpenDOAR (Directory of Open Access Repositories): www.opendoar.org/
11 ROAR (Registry of Open Access Repositories): http://roar.eprints.org/
12 OAIster: www.oaister.org/
13 OAI: www.openarchives.org/
14 BioMed Central: www.biomedcentral.com/
15 DOAJ: www.doaj.org/
16 PLoS: www.publiclibraryofscience.org/
17 PubMed: www.ncbi.nlm.nih.gov/entrez/query.fcgi?db=PubMed
18 PubMed Central: www.pubmedcentral.nih.gov/
19 UK PMC (UK PubMed Central): http://ukpmc.ac.uk/
20 British Library, reports, conferences, and theses: www.bl.uk/services/document/greylit.html
21 GreySource: www.greynet.org/greysourceindex.html
22 BL British Thesis Service: www.bl.uk/services/document/brittheses.html
23 NDLTD: www.ndltd.org/
24 ADT (Australasian Digital Theses Program): http://adt.caul.edu.au/
25 UKDA: www.data-archive.ac.uk/
26 National Geophysical Data Center: www.ngdc.noaa.gov/
27 British Library Conference Collections: www.bl.uk/services/document/conference.html

28 Education Media Online: www.emol.ac.uk/
29 British Library National Sound Archive: www.bl.uk/nsa

Chapter 13

1 Citeulike: www.citeulike.org/
2 LibraryThing: www.librarything.com/

Chapter 14

1 SHERPA/Romeo: www.sherpa.ac.uk/romeo.php
2 UK-IPO: www.ipo.gov.uk/home.htm
3 WIPO: www.wipo.int/madrid/en/members/
4 SPARC Author Addendum: www.arl.org/sparc/author/addendum.html
5 Creative Commons, England & Wales: http://creativecommons.org/license/?jurisdiction=uk
6 Creative Commons Scotland: http://creativecommons.org/worldwide/scotland/
7 Science Commons: http://sciencecommons.org/
8 JISC Plagiarism Advisory Service: www.jiscpas.ac.uk/

Chapter 15

1 Intute: www.intute.ac.uk/
2 SCENTA: www.scenta.co.uk/
3 *Times Higher Education Supplement*: www.thes.co.uk/
4 All Conferences: www.allconferences.com/
5 Conference Alerts: www.conferencealerts.com/
6 Open University Press: http://mcgraw-hill.co.uk/openup/
7 Sage: www.sagepub.co.uk/
8 OUP: www.oup.co.uk
9 Springer Link: www.springerlink.com
10 InformaWorld: www.informaworld.com/
11 InfoTrieve: www4.infotrieve.com/home.asp
12 American Association for the Advancement of Science (AAAS): www.eurekalert.org/
13 Jiscmail: www.jiscmail.ac.uk/
14 LISTERV: www.lsoft.com/

Chapter 16

1 JISC Collections: www.jisc-collections.ac.uk/
2 Alliance for Taxpayer Access: www.taxpayeraccess.org/nih.html
3 JULIET: www.sherpa.ac.uk/juliet/index.php
4 SPARC: www.arl.org/sparc/about/index.html
5 SPARC Europe: www.sparceurope.org/
6 Digital Curation Centre: www.dcc.ac.uk/
7 Research Information Network: www.rin.ac.uk/
8 National e-Science Centre: www.nesc.ac.uk/
9 National Centre for e-Social Science: www.ncess.ac.uk
10 OpCit: Open Citation Project: www.ecs.soton.ac.uk/research/projects/OpCit

Appendix 1

1 The London Library: www.londonlibrary.co.uk/
2 British Library catalogues: www.bl.uk/catalogues/listings.html
3 COPAC: www.copac.ac.uk/copac/

Appendix 2

1 ZETOC: http://zetoc.mimas.ac.uk/
2 Royal Geographical Society: www.rgs.org
3 British Geological Survey: www.bgs.ac.uk/products/digitalmaps/home.html
4 Library of Congress: www.loc.gov/rr/microform/
5 Intute: www.intute.ac.uk/

Index

Related books from Open University Press
Purchase from www.openup.co.uk or order through your local bookseller

HOW TO RESEARCH
Third Edition

Loraine Blaxter, Christina Hughes and Malcolm Tight

Praise for the first edition:

> . . . an excellent choice for any student about to start a research project for the first time.
>> *British Journal of Educational Technology*

Praise for the second edition:

> *How to Research* is best used as a reference tool to dip in and out of when required. Not only is it an excellent starting point for new researchers and students, but undoubtedly the more experienced researcher will also find it valuable. Furthermore, those involved in teaching research methods or supervising research students would find this a useful source of information, exercises and ideas.
>> *SRA News*

How to Research is a practical handbook for those carrying out small scale research projects and discusses the practice and experience of doing research in the social sciences.

The new edition has been updated throughout and includes extensively revised chapters on introductory thinking about research and data analysis. Building on the strengths of the previous edition, Blaxter, Hughes and Tight include new material on:

- Writing research proposals
- Making presentations
- Researching in your own workplace
- Data collection software and time management
- Case studies of small scale research projects

It is written in an original, accessible and jargon free style using a variety of different forms of presentation to support the researcher. It is written for all those who are required to complete a research project as part of their studies and is invaluable for those conducting research in the workplace.

Contents
List of boxes – All at sea but learning to swim – Getting started – Thinking about methods – Reading for research – Managing your project – Collecting data – Analysing data – Writing up – Finishing off – References – Index.

2006 304pp
978–0–335–21746–5 (Paperback)   978–0–335–21747–2 (Hardback)

THE RESEARCH STUDENT'S GUIDE TO SUCCESS
Third Edition

Pat Cryer

A must read for all research students!

> The core material in Professor Cryer's previous editions is classic. I welcome this new edition setting it into current contexts.
>
> *PhD supervisor*

> When I was doing my own PhD, Pat Cryer's book was my constant reference companion. Now I am recommending her latest edition to my own students.
>
> *PhD supervisor*

Insightful, wide-ranging and accessible, this is an invaluable tool for postgraduate research students and for students at all levels working on research projects, irrespective of their field of study.

This edition has been thoroughly revised to accommodate the changes in postgraduate education over recent years. Additional material and new emphases take into account:

- the QAA Code of Practice for Postgraduate Research Programmes
- recommendations of the Roberts Review
- the needs of the growing number of 'overseas' research students
- employment issues (including undergraduate teaching)
- the Internet as a resource for research.

There are new chapters on:

- developing the research proposal
- succeeding as an 'overseas' research student
- ethics in research
- personal development planning (PDP)

Contents

List of figures – Preface to the third edition – Why and how to use this book – Exploring routes, opportunities and funding – Making an application – Producing the research proposal – Settling in and taking stock – Interacting with supervisors – Reading round the subject: working procedures – Reading round the subject: evaluating quality – Handling ethical issues – Managing influences of personal circumstances – Succeeding as an 'overseas' research student – Managing your skills development – Planning out the work – Getting into a productive routine – Co-operating with others for mutual support – Producing progress reports – Giving presentations on your work – Transferring registration from MPhil to PhD – Coming to terms with originality in research – Developing ideas through creative thinking – Keeping going when you feel like giving up – Job seeking – Producing the thesis – Handling the oral/viva/thesis defence – Afterwards! – Appendix: Skills training requirements for research students: Joint Statement by the UK Research Councils – Index.

2006   288pp
978–0–335–22117–2 (Paperback)   978–0–335–22118–9 (Hardback)

THE GOOD RESEARCH GUIDE
FOR SMALL-SCALE RESEARCH PROJECTS
Third Edition

Martyn Denscombe

As a best-selling introductory book on the basics of social research, *The Good Research Guide* provides an accessible yet comprehensive introduction to the main approaches to social research and the methods most commonly used by researchers in the social sciences.

This edition has been updated to account for recent developments in the field such as:

- The emergence of mixed methods approaches
- Increased use of internet research
- More frequent use of methods such as triangulation and focus groups
- Developments in research ethics

Written for anyone undertaking a small-scale research project, either as part of an academic course or as part of their professional development, this book provides:

- A clear, straightforward introduction to data collection methods and data analysis
- Explanations of the key decisions researchers need to take, with practical advice on how to make appropriate decisions
- Essential checklists to guide good practice

This book is perfect for the first-time researcher looking for guidance on the issues they should consider and traps they should avoid when embarking on a social research project.

Contents
*List of figures – Acknowledgements – Introduction – **Part 1: Strategies for social research** – Surveys – Case studies – Experiments – Ethnography – Phenomenology – Grounded theory – Mixed research – Action research – **Part 2: Methods of social research** – Questionnaires – Interviews – Observation – Documents – **Part 3: Analysis** – Quantitative data – Qualitative data – Writing up your research – Frequently asked questions – References – Index.*

2007   360pp
978–0–335–22022–9 (Paperback)

UNIVERSITY OF WOLVERHAMPTON
LEARNING & INFORMATION SERVICES